The Not-So Right Way to Survive Cancer: Part Two

Written By
Jay Libby

Edited By
Jay and Renee Libby

Cover Art By
Jay Libby

The Not-So Right Way to Survive Cancer© 2009 Jason Libby

This book is protected under copyright laws of the United States of America.

Printed in the U.S.A.

Sale of this book without its cover is not authorized by the publisher. If you purchased this book without a cover, you should be aware that neither the author nor the publisher has received payment for this "stripped" book.

Dilly Green Bean Games
Gorham, ME

Visit us online at: www.dillygreenbeangames.com

Abstract

Welcome to my story. It is a true tale of survival. But unlike other such tales of cancer, this is the raw truth. This is how it happened. You are going to experience it all and when you finish reading you will either love me or hate me. This wasn't an easy story to tell. I spent three years picking away at my memoir. I had to sort out fantasy from reality. It was hard to do considering I had lost my memory during the time this all took place. But through friends and music I was able to put it all together.

What you will be reading is the second half of a much larger piece. I have tried to explain the characters and reintroduce places as needed. I have been accused of "putting on a show" in this piece. It's been said that in real life people don't act the way I did. But when you are facing death and Errol Flynn is your childhood idol, you tend to live as far on the edge as possible.

Acknowledgements

I need to thank Dianne Benedict, who gave me the chance to prove people wrong about my writing.

To Richard Hoffman and Baron Wormser who showed me the path to enlightenment.

The staff at Mercy Hospital and NIH for keeping my sorry butt alive.

To my friends and family.

But most of all, this book is for all those who didn't survive.

The Not-So Right Way to Survive Cancer: Part Two

So you want to know what it's like to have cancer? Got that curious urge? Maybe a sick twisted need to know the truth? Well here is the real deal. No angels, no religion, no sappy crap, just hard reality. You aren't going to like what you read, but you'll keep reading because it's all here. Drugs, intrigue and of course…..sex. It's a once in a lifetime experience and you have the front row seat.

Before you start reading you need a little back story. In 1995, I was stationed in Ingleside, Texas, home to rattlesnakes, oil refineries and a Navy shipyard. A massive chemical spill and a lung full of toxins landed me with cancer. I had my chest cracked open and went through regular CHOP chemotherapy. I thought I was in remission. I went back to the Navy and got stationed in Portland, Maine. But with all things in life, it wasn't that easy. I was about to get one hell of a reality check.

Disclaimer

Some names have been changed in this book to protect people. Other names are real. This book is NOT for children or anyone under 17 years of age. It involves serious topics and very questionable behavior. My survival was unique and not recommended as a solid medical protocol. So why write about it? Because the most messed up things can change you and survival comes from attitude.

Table of Contents

The Second Great Smack			Page 6

Betrayal, Fresh Starts and Sin		Page 11

Misery Likes Company			Page 48

Countdown to Death			Page 75

The Second Great Smack

It was December 1996 when I smoked my first joint. I did it for Dawn. It's one of those crazy ideas that you indulge because you think the girl you've been in love with and shaking up the bed with will love you more. She smoked pot once and a while and her dad was an avid fan of the green. I had been cancer free for almost 3 months and I felt that it was my God given right to smoke it up even if I was still in the Navy. Dawn made me feel evil, so evil that I had unclean thoughts every time I looked at her. And man did she like to fuck. You name it and we were doing it. In the car and in the parking garage. She gave me road blows while her brother was riding in the back seat. It was every guy's dream. I was a beast and she was my beauty in bed. The relationship was all about sex. I don't even know how she really felt about me, but I worked on her. Tried to win her heart. She even moved in with me. When we walked side by side I towered over her. She was short, not thin, but average in size. I remember her breasts were perfect hand sized. As a kid I remember all my classmates drooling over her when she moved to Maine from Pennsylvania. That was back in eighth grade. Guys talking about how they wanted to grab her boobs. I was so scared of girls back then that I never thought about her. But the Navy changed me. We hooked up at the premiere of *Star Trek: First Contact*. After the film was over we hopped right into bed, no questions asked. Not bad for a first date. From that point on it was all about the sex. With cancer out of the picture I was back to being an ego driven, sex crazed maniac. It was good. Evenings spent watching Dawn's shadow on the wall, her short brown hair bouncing back and forth, her body doing the dance.

The night I smoked it was stormy. Snow hammered down on my little red Mazda. It wasn't meant for that type of weather, but its little tires held tight on the road. Dawn's father was living with a family on the outskirts of Riverside in Portland, near the industrial park by the train tracks. It was a two story house, with a driveway running along the side. Its white exterior blended nicely with the winter scene. The whole family was festively plump, nice people. I really felt like they were my extended family. Dawn's father was a thin scruffy looking fellow who spent his whole life doing manual labor for lack of a decent education. He was a hard worker, and a pothead all the way to the bone.

We pulled up in my little red Mazda MX3. The snow was blowing everywhere and Dawn quickly jumped out of the car and ran inside. I sat there and wondered where the hell she was going. She didn't say a word to me. I walked inside and the father of the family was sitting there in a chair and he told me that Dawn was with her dad in the living room smoking one. He offered me a drink and I declined. Dawn was already working away on a joint. She looked like a pothead alright. Her cheeks puffing heavily and her eyes rolling back. The room itself was dark, with the Christmas tree lights blinking away at the other side. My form flickered on the walls. I sat next to Dawn on the couch with her father on the other side.

"Jay, wanna try some?" he asked as he took a deep drag from the joint, the end glowing bright red, almost like Rudolph's red nose.

"He can't, Daddy." Dawn cut in. "He's in the Navy."

"You know what? Fuck it." I reached over and swiped a fresh joint from the coffee table that was covered in wrappers, weed, zip lock baggies, and an ashtray. Dawn tried to take it from me, but I pushed her back. "What, you can smoke it but I can't?"

"But what about the drug testing?" Dawn tried once again to steal it from me.

"Girl, who the fuck do you think sets up the drug testing?" I smirked and Dawn's father tossed me a lighter.

"Smoke it up, Jay." Her dad laughed. At that moment I lost my innocence. With that single drag I corrupted myself further than I'd ever done before. I was now a hypocrite. Anti-drug my ass. Here I was smoking it. The one thing I swore I'd never do. My Grandpa Parker must have cast me out from his view from Heaven that night. At first nothing happened. I sat there and literally sucked the whole thing down, really burned through that shit. Dawn and her father just looked at me in awe.

"Have you ever smoked this shit before?" Her dad chuckled.

"I have smoked lots of things, including your daughter." Holy fuck, I had totally just screwed the pooch. The pot had taken its hold. I'd just told my girlfriend's dad that I had been smoking his little girl. I smiled my devil's grin, the one that Lucifer himself had given me. The world changed in a flash. Dawn's dad stood up, reached for me and flipped his hand over.

"Fuck'n right! I like a guy with balls, even if he's banging them off my little girl's ass." I reached my hand out and he gave me five. Ok, that sounds really fucked up, but he was so stoned I don't think he would have known any different. As for myself, I gave Dawn a kiss and rolled off the couch and onto the floor. My head fell with a soft thud. The brown carpet was thick. My body was at ease.

"Hey, come here." I crawled over to the Christmas tree and flipped onto my back, placing my head under the tree and the lights. Dawn joined me. We looked up at the blinking lights past the shadows bouncing off the ceiling. I remember it well because the house had a textured ceiling that looked like scales hanging in stasis. I giggled and held Dawn's hand. "I love you."

***

Speed ahead a few weeks past Christmas.

"I'm moving in with Kristen, but I still want to see you." Dawn had a look of primal guilt. She wouldn't make eye contact with me. I reached out and took Dawn's arm.

"Let go of her arm, Jay!" Kristen barked at me. Her face was carved in stone. Her nails clawed into my wrist.

"You see, you are controlling." Dawn raised her nose at me like some type of rich bitch.

"What the fuck is going on here?" I asked myself aloud as I stood in the kitchen with a towel around my waist and my hand clenching Dawn's arm. In a matter of seconds I watched my girlfriend move out without any notice or anything. This must have been planned long before that day. Kristen was a bisexual chick who loved to fuck with my head and didn't care for me at all. She had been filling Dawn's head with shit since they started hanging out. But to move Dawn out while I was in the shower and not even say goodbye was fucked up. So here I was, half naked confronting both women.

"Controlling my ass! What the fuck is happening here?" I held my towel tight.

"I just want to move out. But we are still dating, don't worry." I could see Dawn was not all with it.

"Look you wife beater, let her go." Kristen smacked my hand and I let go of Dawn. "See Dawn, he is physically violent, he grabbed you."

I shook my head in disbelief. This was all really happening. Dawn was walking right out of my life just as fast as she had come in. I watched her walk out the door. The first thought that came to my mind was I wanted to die. I had beaten cancer only to get fucked by this bitch. This was how God was punishing me.

***

The next week was hell. I ended up sitting in the Emergency Room at Mercy Hospital feeling suicidal, Chief Johnson sat with me. The Chief was really cool. Ever since I had gotten stationed at the reserve center on Commercial Street he had been like a father figure to me. We used to joke that I was his white shadow. My orders even said I specifically answered only to him. It was a tight friendship and my loyalty to him was unbreakable. I would have taken a bullet for this guy.

"I'm sorry she hurt you, Libby." Chief patted me on my back. "But there are plenty of girls out there. She isn't worth it."

"I know, it just hurts how this all happened. I feel like the bad-guy here and I'm not even sure why." I thought about where I was. Next week I was due at the Naval Hospital in Bethesda, Maryland for my medical follow-up. "Shit, let's bail Chief. I need to be in DC next week, I can't get committed." It was a hard choice for me. Get mental help and miss my appointment, or go to DC and see if I'm well enough to get myself shot.

"Are you sure?" Chief looked a little skeptical.

"Yeah, I have been through cancer, I can go through this." With that we got up and left Mercy.

***

I sat there in disbelief. I was angry. I was so pissed off. Doctor Shapiro just stood there with my scans. It was welcome news in some ways. I could finally just die in peace.

"There is a tumor the size of a quarter in your left lung. The CHOP therapy didn't work. Your body fought the drugs."

"So am I going to die?"

"Without treatment you will for sure. But because CHOP didn't work we can only offer you a few options."

"Like?"

"Well there is salvage CHOP, a bone marrow transplant, this new study at The National Institute of Health or no treatment at all."

"What are odds of surviving with salvage?"

"40%"

"And with this new chemo?"

"30%"

"And I know what my odds are with a bone marrow transplant. Shitty."

"Pretty much."

"Well then, fuck you doc. I will take the no treatment option and just leave." I jumped up off the table and buttoned up my shirt. Doctor Shapiro tried to step in front of me as I went to leave. "Get the fuck out of my way or they'll be cleaning you off of the walls." I gave him a look of death. At that moment I felt like I could kill anyone who got in my way and I was ready to do it. Doctor Shapiro backed away and I stormed into the hall. Several of my shipmates heard the yelling and came to rescue the doctor, but he was safe. I had other priorities.

Sullivan grabbed my arm. "Jesus, Libby. Where do you think you're going?"

"I am going to go somewhere and die. Got a fucking problem with that?"

"You can't. As a member of the armed services you can't refuse treatments. I'll stop you if I have to."

I looked at Tara Sullivan. She was so beautiful to me. She had always been a good friend and I valued that. Tara could have passed as a Tonya Harding clone. I shut down my Kill Mode, but continued down the white hallway and out into the elevators. Tara followed me, trying to convince me to stop. But her voice was lost to me. I was heading to my death.

"The only way to stop me is to call the shore patrol on my ass." No sooner had those words left my lips, the elevator doors opened and two armed shore patrol officers stepped towards me. I was ready to die. Then reality hit, I was screwed.

Betrayal, Fresh Starts and Sin

Life deals you shitty situations all the time. Sometimes you suck it up, other times it keeps just pissing on you when you are down. Dawn wasn't done fucking with me. We met at Kristen's house shortly after she had moved out. I was there to see where we stood. Was I in for a kicker.

"How did your appointment go in DC?" Like she fucking cared.

"I have cancer again and will be going back soon to have another tumor removed this time from my left lung."

"I can't do this."

Here it comes.

"I want to have kids and a family. You're sterile. I emotionally can't handle being with someone with cancer."

Peachy. "Excuse me?" I felt about as little as a piece of dirt in a pile of dog crap.

"I hope you understand, Jay. I do care about you." Dawn's voice was so hollow.

Caring. What the hell does that mean anyway? Seriously. My entire life all I ever heard from girlfriends was the classic 'Oh, I care.' My ass. Ladies, don't kid yourselves. When you say you care you are almost no better than the player who fucks your little sister and says he cares while he is out banging his buddy's ex. I hate the word "care". So much that when I say I care, I actually make sure I mean it. No games. I care about a lot of people, and others I'd gladly put a gun in their sad little hands and encourage them to commit suicide. But hey, that's just me. The super nice, super bastard. It takes talent to be like me. As for Dawn and her 'caring', it was all just some lesbian ploy schemed by Kristen, that's my opinion.

"Oh well, they said there was an 80% chance I'd die anyway." I was happy about that number. I was going to die. Good, I really needed it. "Good luck with your life. Be happy."

And that was it. No more Dawn in my life.

***

In your life you should always take the chance to do something really off the wall. Some people take up surfing, others sky diving and some even take up ritual murders. Either way it's something totally different. Clinical studies are like that. A patient who is going to die signs up for a dangerous human trail, and data is collected as long as the patient is alive. It means others may live if all goes well and death if things didn't. One of those opportunities came knocking for me. Or I should say I was being groomed to take part in a study that would go down in history as the cancer protocol that killed everyone, except myself. The National Institute of Health had been working with Navy doctors in procuring cancer patients for this research. Doctor Wyndham Wilson of NIH was heading the ground breaking protocol coded EPOCH II. The study was closing, but for some reason I was shifted to the head of a LONG waiting list. The offer was pretty low key. Doctor Shapiro called me at home, told me about the study and wanted an answer right then and there. I was ready to die so I agreed. The basic understanding I have of EPOCH II was this: In regular EPOCH therapy. The patient is given a double dose of the EPOCH protocol which is used for bone marrow transplants. All the cells in your body die and then they implant you with new bone marrow cells which grow. In EPOCH II, you are given double the dosage of these EPOCH drugs and not given a bone marrow transplant. Instead they pump you full of Neupogen and hope that your body will kick-start itself. The long term effect is that the cancer cells will not be able to reproduce anymore. From my understanding there were around 90 patients in this study according to NIH. I was lucky to get the chance I did, even if it was a death sentence.

***

When you're facing death you tend to not care about anything. There is that word again. Care. Who cares? After I soaked up the whole death situation, and Dawn's bullshit, I needed to vent. What better way to do it than to hit the mall and look for a girl to have sex with? If I was going to go it would be with a smile. The first place I hit was Orange Julius, a food stop in the mall where Tiff, a friend of Dawn's, worked.

"Hey, Jay. Sorry about Dawn."

"It's ok, now I am just going to try to get laid before I leave for DC."

When I said that a short girl with an Orange Julius hat pulled over her brow turned and smiled at me. She had long blonde hair and cute cheeks, both front and back.

"Oh really?"

"Why not? If I am going to die from cancer, I want to get it on as much as I can before I die."

"There's nothing wrong with that," she responded.

"Jay, this is Leanna." Tiff interrupted.

"Nice to meet you, wanna have sex?" Yes, I really asked. Don't ask me why. This girl was young, maybe sixteen. I was twenty-one. But you don't think about these things when you are told you are going to die. What came next shocked the hell out of me.

"Sure, pick me up at 9pm out front." She winked.

Tiff looked at me and shook her head. I know what she must have been thinking. Part of me was thinking the same thing. Jail bait. Trouble. Yet, this girl's smile and devilish look drew me in and I was in no mental condition to balance good and evil.

That was Super Bowl Sunday, 1997. A day that up until I met my wife, Leanna and I celebrated even after we broke up four years later. That evening we drove around and talked about her life, her alcoholic father and her mother. Then I drove her to a party where her boyfriend was. There were no adults at this apartment in Portland's East End. It was full of teens smoking weed and drinking. I had partly decided to tip off the cops about this whole thing, but backed off when I realized I was in the thick of it. Leanna's boyfriend was a scrawny preppy kid who had apparently been raping a twelve year old in a back room before we'd arrived. Leanna walked in, look around, and laughed. Before I knew it I was waiting in the car and she was coming back out.

"Hey, I didn't know you had a boyfriend." I shook my head.

"Well he's been cheating on me for weeks now. So I told him that you were DEA and I just fucked you. So they are trying to clean up before the cops arrive."

"Oh Jesus, why the hell did you say that to him?"

"Because I like you and he's a dick. You actually treat me better than he does and I've only known you for a couple hours."

"Um, yeah. I'll bring you home now."

The drive to her house was weird. She took me inside to meet her mother. Brenda was a slender woman with long blonde hair, but she looked nothing like Leanna. When I walked through the door she gave me an insane look. It was one of those busted looks. I was going to jail.

"Ok buddy, driver's license please." Brenda reached her hand out waiting to see my ID.

"I left it at home."

"Mom, cut it out. Jay is cool. He's 18." Leanna loved to lie. And she was good at it. "And he's in the Navy."

"What rank?"

"E-3, ma'am."

"And you're 18?"

"Yes, if you want I can show you my driver's license later."

"Next time I see you, I want a copy of your birth certificate."

Now this all happened in the first night of meeting Leanna. I quickly searched for a response to Brenda's demand. "That might be hard, because of my clearance. My certificate has been marked classified." What a lame excuse, there was no way she would believe it.

"Well you'd better find some way to show me or else I'll forbid you to see my daughter."

"For one, I just gave her a ride home. Second, I'm not interested in dating your daughter. She's nice, but a little too young." That was the honest truth. I didn't want to date anyone or fall for anyone. I was going to be going through hell and then death. The last thing I wanted was a relationship.

"So what is it you want?"

Leanna looked a little heart broken.

"I would like permission to take Leanna out to the movies and dinner while I am home and after I return from DC."

"And what is in DC?"

From here the dialog went into a recap of my cancer history. Brenda understood and by the end of the LONG story, she was cool with me.

"Just remember, don't touch my daughter and don't try to get into her pants, or else."

Leanna smiled, hugged my arm and winked at me when her mother wasn't looking.

***

When I left for DC Leanna saw me off. It was quaint. This time around I didn't suffer through the medical procedures like I had before. No needles in my groin, no med students watching, no wisecracks about what evil lurks in the hearts of men. It was a straight admission into the hospital, but with one exception. I had a sitter, a Petty Officer by the name of Eilley. This was the result of a Senatorial inquiry by Senator Olympia Snowe after I blew the whistle on the horrid conditions of the Naval hospital. Eilley was interesting. I sat in a small cubical with him as he asked me tons of questions. Mostly he wanted to know how I liked the new accommodations. See, this time around I was getting a nice plush hotel room, funded by the Navy. In addition, Eilley going to be my personal babysitter of sorts. But I wasn't complaining. There are some people you just bond with really well. This married sailor with kids, who was about a foot shorter than me and, sporting a traditional Navy mustache, was a good man. I remember sitting there at his desk while he grilled me. He spoke long enough that his screen saver kicked on.

Godzilla? Yes, that radioactive gargantuan who trashed Tokyo at least 3 times a month, was now scrolling across his screen. But I hadn't seen this Godzilla before.

"Wow, is that new?"

"The computer?"

"No, Godzilla."

"Yeah, these are stills from the new series that Toho released."

"I've never seen a Godzilla that cool except in Godzilla 1985."

"These films are sequels. I have a bunch on tape."

"Damn, where can I get them?"

"I'll tell you what, I'll make sure you get a TV and VCR in your room after they slice your lung. You can watch them all."

"Are you serious?" Ok, now this guy was getting my attention.

"Yeah, no problem at all. After your letter to the Senator they authorized me to pamper you. I figured I would maybe visit you, but hey, if you dig the lizard we might end up being good friends."

"Well don't kiss my ass, you out rank me. I joined for tradition, leave me that."

"Not many people dig Godzilla. So we need to keep a tight ship with fans."

"Well, I appreciate it."

"No problem. The first three films have subtitles, the others, however, are in Japanese with no translation. I'll even throw in the new Gamera film."

"Sweet." It was an odd feeling. Not having a gut reaction to getting shafted.

***

The lecture I got from the Admiral this time was pretty much the same. She told me that they were going to go in and take a wedge from my left lung. If the docs couldn't get to it, they would have to crack my chest open again. I wouldn't know until I woke up. So once again I had to shave my chest, sign those damn papers and generally feel like crap. Sergio and Jen, shipmates who over the last year had become more like family, and who'd stood by me the first time I went through all this, were by my side yet again. Sergio kept pointing out all the new asses on the floor, winking at me every time one walked by. His dark Mediterranean skin kept prompting my imagination to picture him on a beach somewhere with loads of gals dancing the night away. Jen had lost weight since I had last seen her, but the curves were still there and her round face was still enthralling. Even her hair had style, with medium black strands pulled back into a military uniform code. We had grown apart, but this time around she was in my room with me a lot. I guess she had some feelings for me, but I was ready to die. Jen, Sergio, Mom, Dad, Leanna, and anyone else who were part of my life couldn't save me. I would have kicked Leanna to the curb in a heartbeat if Jen had been more open with me. But fear tends to seal lips. My friends and shipmates didn't know what to say to me. Before I went down the hall of lights, like last time, I gave them both big hugs. They were my family away from home. I loved them.

When I awoke from surgery I was in a large recovery room. I had tubes hanging from my chest and my left side. My vision was blurry, but I managed to glance down. No tape. My left hand tried to move and a nurse grabbed me. "Don't move! You need to wake up more."

"Please, I am the guy whose body resisted chemo. Did they crack me?"

"Nope, they got part of your lung though."

"Umm, no kidding sweetheart."

I was relieved. If my chest had been re-cracked it would have meant more rehab and months of pain. I was quick to come out of recovery, like that was any surprise. I don't remember much. But I do remember two very important events that occurred after they brought me back to the regular floor.

The first was the breathing machine and the treatment that accompanied it. When you have your chest cracked, or half-lung surgery, the doctors make you use an inspirator to strengthen your lungs The treatment started on what was a typical day for me. I was sitting in bed watching TV as the hustle and bustle of the Navy Hospital spiraled around me. An Air Force Major interrupted my peace.

"Fireman Libby?" This stout fellow dressed in a flight surgeon's uniform stood in my room next to a large breathing machine made of tubs and tanks.

"Yes?" I looked at him.

"Time for your breathing treatment."

"Ok. Let's do this." I sat up in my bed and prepared myself. My chest tubes were dangling out of my left side and lower chest.

"Ok. What I want you to do is breath deep into the machine." The Major waved a face mask and slid it over my mouth and nose.

"Sure." I wasn't pleased. There was precious little time I got to myself, and now this Major was totally messing it up. I watched as he turned a nozzle on his machine and gave me a thumb's up. I took a large breath in. It felt like I was drowning. My left lung began to spasm and I started to cough.

"Take another deep breath." The Major ordered.

I couldn't. I began to gasp for air, and my coughing increased. My side began to ache and before I could do anything about it there was a massive burst in my side. Fluids from my side chest tube sprayed across the room onto the curtain and the wall. The Major fell backwards into a chair.

"Oh my God!" He screamed.

I acted quickly and stuck my thumb into my side, plugging the hole. "Aren't you going to do something?" I looked at the Major who was now green in the face. Then in a split instant I saw JG, my officer nurse. "JG, I need your help here."

"What is it?" JG peaked in and her eyes bugged out. "Holy shit!"

"Yeah, I was thinking the same thing." I smiled. JG was good. She pushed the Major aside and grabbed a kit from a drawer next to my bed. Wrappers flew as she dug for gauze and upon finding it, slapped it over my thumb.

"When I tell you to pull your thumb out." JG winked.

"Yes, Ma'am."

"Now!"

I removed my thumb from between my ribs and JG packed the gaping hole full of gauze. My thumb was yellow and bloody. I heard a voice over all the commotion.

"When can we reschedule?" The Major whispered.

"Reschedule? Get the hell out of here!" JG snapped at him, sending the man who was responsible for me losing a chest tube scampering out of my room.

"Thanks, JG."

"No problem. But now we have a spot here. Do we do another tube?"

"No thanks. I have had enough action for today."

"Well we might as well pull the two front ones." JG started getting ready for some fun.

"Great." I frowned. It was like having the life sucked out of me.

***

The second great event began with a midnight walk to the X-ray department. Because the hospital had been slammed all day, I ended up going for a routine chest x-ray at midnight. A corpsman offered to walk with me, but hey, I'm Jay. I can soak up pain like it's going out of style. I marched my pajama'd butt down the empty hallways of the Naval hospital. Except for a few wayward patients out for an evening walk I was alone. The waiting area for the x-ray department looked like an airport. There were large benches everywhere, digital numbering systems to let you know when you were up. The red dots, glowing like devils, looking down upon me. This late at night there was no line. Not a soul. I approached the darkened desk and smacked a small bell harder than it needed to be to draw attention to myself.

"Fireman Libby?" a voice echoed in the empty waiting area. A large wooden door to my right opened and a corpsman wearing scrubs waved for me to follow her.

"Dead in here, huh?" I winked at the girl. She was a bit large for Navy, but then again, nothing surprised me these days.

"It's midnight. What do you expect?" She pulled a large bib from the wall. It looked weighted and the green did not compliment my baby blue pajamas. "Put this on."

"What for?" I put my hand out and raised my palm flat in her direction.

"I don't have time for these foolish games. Put it on now! That's an order." Yep. Orders. She had to get all military on me. But I could respect that. Well only so much. I was still very sore from the chest tube blow the day before. Not having all of both lungs tends to make even the easiest task feel like a bloody ten mile hump through the jungle.

"It's on. Now what?" I asked very sarcastically. The corpsman tugged me around and placed me in front of a standing bull's eye. "Mmmm. Gonna shoot me?" I chuckled.

"No, wiseass. I am going to take an x-ray." She barked.

"Bad day?" I inquired, trying to be nice.

"You ever have one of those days where people just piss you off?" She vented.

"I'm a Hull Tech. I get pissed on every day." I responded. "And I have cancer. But hey, shit happens right?"

She looked at me for a second. Her angry cheeks turned to a smile. She walked over to me and stared. She went over my face inch by inch. "Cancer?"

"Twice now. But I still put on my uniform and still carry on. Why piss it away on the petty stuff?" I reached out and rubbed her arm. The corpsman just stood there. I think it was shock. "Nothing like getting nuked on the first date. Light me up."

Her face was now one of joy. Whatever had been eating at her was no longer ruling her morning. "Fireman Libby, thank you."

"Hey, we're shipmates. It's what we're here for." I faced the target and waited for the instructions.

"Take a deep breath, hold it." The corpsman's voice was now a beautiful sound. I did as she told me. After the click, she pulled the film and went into another room.

A couple minutes passed. I was alone in a room full of x-ray equipment. Alone.

"I'm sorry, we need to do one more." She came back with fresh film.

I assumed the position and awaited the instruction. "Take a deep breath."

At the full extent that my lung could fill I heard a popping sound. A loud one. "Did you hear that?"

"It must have been the machine." The corpsman took her picture and retrieved the film yet again.

"I felt it in my chest." The pain was quick. It didn't last more than an instant.

"Just let the nurse know when you get upstairs." And that was the end of our conversation.

I stood in the elevator. Alone. The x-rays done. The lights flickered as it started going up. Piano music. First floor. Second floor. Third floor. Pain in my left lung. Fourth floor. Unimaginable pain in my left lung. No air. I was suffocating. The elevator door slid open. I stepped forward trying to breath. Gasping, but no air. My left side was pulsing. Massive pain. I stumbled past the gumball machine and down the hallway. The empty hallway. I composed myself as I got closer to the nurse's station. The hallway went from being dim to being well lit. A nurse sat at the desk reading a book. When I opened my mouth to get her attention nothing came out. I began to stagger again and slammed my body up against the counter in front of her.

"How'd it go?" She smiled. "Why is your face purple?" The nurse set her book down and looked at me. She looked at me like I was seriously screwed. "Fireman Libby?"

"Lung, popped." That was all I could manage to get out of my mouth. The last of my air was gone. I was unable to take in air. Unable to survive.

"Popped? Oh my GOD!" She jumped up and hit a button under the counter. A light flashed above the nurse's station.

The room began to spin and all I saw were two corpsman running toward me. Then I heard a really loud crack, as gravity pulled my face into the counter. No air. Darkness. No air. Darkness. No air. Hissing. Bright light. More hissing. Bright light in my right eye. "Jason?" Bright light in my left eye. "Jason wake up!" The suffocating feeling started to fade. "Get me a javelin." I forced my eyes to open. Faces. Many faces. Looking at me like I had coded. "Wait. He's coming around." My lips moved, but my jaw was covered by a face mask. "Jason, can you hear me?" Instead of speaking I just smiled. "He's ok. SATs?" I kept smiling. "Returning to normal. Barely. Keep up the oxygen and give him another five minutes. If the SATs don't go up then we'll do the javelin."

"No javelin." I muttered.

"Jesus, he's speaking!" a voice sounded relieved. "Don't talk too much. You have a pneumothorax. So just keep breathing the oxygen."

I nodded my head and kept breathing. The faces vanished into the night. Finally, I was alone. No javelins. No pain. Just the rush of pure oxygen. And cancer.

***

It was like a dream. I was lost in my thoughts, my eyes closed, and all I could hear was my breathing. Then someone nudged me. At first I felt like just telling whoever it was to piss off. But it didn't feel like the usual wake-up call for vitals at 1700 hours. It had a sneakier feel. Like someone might be trying to cause trouble. I peaked through one eye and saw Jen standing over me.

"I'm here to break you out." She said with her big ole' smile.

"Where's Sergio?"

"He's got duty, so you and I have a date."

Jen and I had been in constant touch during my time away. While we had no relationship, it was still a connection that worked well. When we were apart we had our own lives. But when we were together we were like teen lovers, always looking to sneak away somewhere. It was a surprise to have her at my bedside. I hadn't seen much of her other than the usual passing in the halls of the Naval Hospital.

"Considering it's not winter, I'll take it we are not going ice skating again."

"Nope, I was thinking something more romantic. How about dinner and a movie?" God the thought of a nice romantic evening with Jen was just what I needed. While I had pushed most of my female associates away, Jen was one who could be a serious possibility. Especially if I ended up moving to Bethesda for treatments which was the plan the

Navy had.

"All I have is sweats. I'm afraid it might not be too romantic." I was worried. I would look like I was sick no matter what.

"Don't worry. The date is with you, not your outfit." Jen kissed me on the cheek. This was the second time I had been kissed by Jen. My heart began to pound and I quickly jumped up and got dressed.

"Mr. Libby, where are you going? You have orders to stay put." JG caught me at the door.

"I thought it'd be nice to take Fireman Libby for a walk Ma'am." Jen interrupted.

"Ok, but don't leave the hospital. Not after your lung and your chest tube incident." JG waved us on. "Keep it to the main building."

"Yes Ma'am!" we both saluted and quickly walked past her, hand in hand. I can only image what JG was thinking. Probably thought we were going to go get into trouble. We were.

Escaping the main building was easy. There were over a few thousand patients there. It was not like anybody was watching out for me. Jen and I scurried out one of the doors near the parking garage and headed to the enlisted parking lot.

"We did it!" Jen pulled me close and planted a kiss on my lips. I must have missed something. I didn't think Jen was that interested in me. "I missed you so much!"

"Easy there." I pulled away. "Is everything ok?"

"Yes, now that you're back." Jen walked up to a dark purple sports car and unlocked the passenger door. "Hop in!"

"Sounds like a plan." I carefully ducked down and landed in her passenger seat. "I missed you too, Jen. I never thought we might ever have a real date."

"I did a lot of thinking while you were away. When I heard that you were moving down here I knew that I could open up to you." Now I hadn't told anyone I was moving to Maryland. As a matter of fact, the doctors said it was an option. It was one I hadn't taken. But now that Jen was here and wanting to have something more, reconsideration was part of a new equation. Jen grabbed my hand and squeezed. "You inspire me to live. And I want to help you beat cancer again. We can do it."

"Jen, did I ever tell you that I had a major crush on you?" I smiled.. I felt like I could just let my wall collapse and I did. "Part of me has always loved you. I just didn't think I'd have a chance with you. This feels like one of those old black and white films. You know the ones where the two people meet but life keeps them from being together? This is what we've got."

"But I thought they always ended up together in the end?"

"Not in Casablanca. That movie had the girl leaving with another guy." Jen's hand warmed mine. My skin had been clammy ever since I had my surgery. My body knew what was about to happen. It wanted to quit. But here was Jen, this gal from Wisconsin who made me warm. Her skin on mine. It was not erotic, it was tender. I don't know why Jen came back to me. But it didn't matter. With all the shit I had put up with, Jen was an escape. I loved her.

We went to Bennigan's for supper. It was a common hang out spot. It was also safe. The meal was warm, the alcohol was warmer and my pulse was pounding a mile a minute. Our conversation centered on my life and treatment for my cancer. Jen had versed herself with EPOCH II and found the whole study terrifying. So did I.

"So why don't we get an apartment together before you start treatment? That way I can take care of you between treatments?" It was a funny suggestion, but one I knew made sense.

"I don't see why not? It would give us at least a week together in a normal relationship before I start chemo." It was an easy choice. I would get the girl and I'd get back into the Navy's grace by being in Bethesda. "I'll come back in a few days."

"You will?" Jen sounded surprised. "I thought you weren't able to fly for a month or so?"

"It's called driving. I've got the blood of a race car driver in me. Go go go." I laughed, swigged more of my drink and continued to hold her hand.

"Just don't push yourself too hard. All you need is another bump in the road." Jen smiled once again.

When dinner was finished we drove around for a while. Jen wanted to show me Bethesda and the sites. There was a lot I had never seen. Things like the Discovery Channel Building, the mall, the movie theatres and so on. It was peaceful. The thought crossed my mind about what life would be like with her. If I were to survive, how would we do? Would she want kids? It was a sinking feeling. "Jen, did you ever think about having kids?"

"I have. But if you're implying that I wouldn't want to be with you if you weren't able to, then try again." It was comforting. I honestly felt like she really wanted to be with me.

"Cool, I was just…." My thought was cut short by the impact of a car into the passenger's side of Jen's car. My head smacked against the window and my stitching in my left side tore open. I looked around as the car rolled to a stop. Jen looked at me, checking to see if I was ok.

"What the hell!" Jen shouted. Her car pulled to the side of the road. Another car was stopped in the intersection behind us. The front end of the Jen's compact was pushed in. "I was turning and he ran the light! Jesus, are you ok?"

"I'm good, how about you?" I felt blood running down my side and quickly covered the area where red was soaking through.

"Is your side ok? Let me look!" Jen tried to pull my hand away.

"I'm fine. We need to check on that ass." Jen and I got out of the car. I tried to jump out, but the tear was causing me a lot of pain. I stood by our car as the other driver walked over. The first words out of his mouth weren't in English. Anger boiled inside of me. The next set of words were in broken English. "Great, a fucking immigrant. How the hell did he get a driver's license if he doesn't even speak English?"

Jen started yelling at the man who had no real clue what she was saying. Next thing I knew a set of blue lights started flashing behind me. A police cruiser pulled up and two officers got out. One came over to me and saw a sponge-like red design on the side of Jen's car. He looked at my side which was oozing red.

"Shit kid, you're hurt!" He went for his radio. "I'll call for an ambulance."

"No, don't! I am fine. I don't want her to know. I'm going to the hospital anyway. We work at the Naval Hospital." All I needed is for Jen to get busted for sneaking a prisoner, I mean patient, out.

"Ok, but get that patched up soon." The officer headed over to Jen and the offending driver, both of whom were yelling back and forth.

The next twenty minutes sucked. What a way to end a romantic evening. Jen wasn't at fault and her car was still drivable. The other guy? Well the cops took him away in handcuffs. I didn't give a shit about what they did with him.

On the way back Jen was a wreck. "Oh my god. I snuck you out and we got in an accident. They are going to notice that bump on your head."

"It's all good. I'll take care of this. Just calm down." I reached over and held her hand with my blood soaked hand.

"Why is your hand wet?" Jen looked down. "Oh shit, you're bleeding! I need to stitch you up. Why didn't you say anything back there?"

"Because I know how this will look if you bring me back all fucked up. The cops know, but there is no need for the Navy to." I opened her glove compartment and pulled out a box of tissues. The blood didn't wipe away easily. Tissues turn into pieces of messy crud when you try to wipe anything sticky with them.

"What happens if it is something more serious?" Jen started to cry.

I leaned over and kissed her cheek. "I'll take care of it." Just like she wanted to take care of me.

When we got back to the hospital I gave Jen a really good kiss goodnight and snuck across the Quarterdeck with a newspaper against my left side. The watch didn't see the blood and I was able to quickly get onto the elevator. When I reached my unit I ducked inside the kitchen and looked around. I needed to cover for Jen. What could I do? There were some loose trays and a couple empty boxes on the floor. I pulled the trays out far enough so that they were hanging over the edge of the counter. I raised my hands up and with all my might smashed them down, sending the trays flying into the air. There was a tremendous crash and I fell onto the floor. Two corpsmen came running in to investigate. I laid there with my hand on my side. Blood started oozing again. It was perfect.

"What happened?" asked one corpsman as she ran to where I was laying.

"I tripped over that box and hit my head on those trays. I think I tore out my stitches too." I began to cry. Not because it was so funny, but because the pain in my head and side was becoming uncontrollable. I was taken out on a stretcher and brought to X-Ray where they checked my head for fractures. The stitches in my side were replaced. That night I slept well. Pumped full of pain meds and dreams of Jen.

***

The next day JG came in to see me. She didn't look happy. "I see you managed to get hurt last night. Did this happen while you were out with the corpsman or did it really happen here?"

"It happened here, Ma'am." I smiled.

"Let me remind you that you are a patient and that I am the nurse. I read the report from last night. Tripped on a box and hit your head on a dozen trays?" JG shook her head. "The corpsman who stitched you said that the stitches looked like they had been torn out prior to the fall."

"Well that's what happened. What do you want me to say? Oops?" I smiled, but JG didn't.

"You are the property of the US Navy. If you are lying I can send you to Captain's Mass." It was a threat that I knew she wouldn't do. "When you go home this week I expect you to stay home and recover."

"Actually Ma'am, I plan on coming back sooner so I can get situated. I'm looking at getting an apartment."

"With that girl right? That is a bad idea. You are going to be very sick. From what I understand you'll be spending every two weeks in the hospital." JG shook her head and waved her finger at me.

"Whatever. Last time I did just fine. And I think that 'girl' would be just fine taking care of me. Last time I knew the Navy couldn't control my love life."

"We can't, but we sure the hell can make it impossible!" JG stood up and stormed out.

Jen didn't come to see me until later in the day. It was my last day at the hospital before I went home for my rest and relaxation. When she walked in she did it covertly. I went to say 'hello' and she quickly raised her index finger to her lips. "Shhhh."

"I can't stay long." She kissed my lips and gave me a long hug. "So what happened when you got back?"

"Not much. I created a big scene and they fell for it. Are you ok?"

"My neck hurts, but that's it. I am glad to see you're alright."

"Yep. So how do you want to plan my return?" Jen pulled out a piece of paper with a listing of apartments for rent.

"Here is a list of apartments that we can afford. Most are right here in Bethesda." Jen showed me the ones she really wanted to look into.

"Cool. I'll drive down in a couple days and we'll move."

"Great." Jen hugged me, careful not to pull on my side.

"Ah-hum!" The voice was all too familiar. It was JG. "Now I know what is going on. Corpsman, come with me please! You two, watch him." Two corpsman came into the room and stood there. Jen walked out looking terrified.

The wait seemed like an eternity. I twiddled my thumbs for a bit. Then I began to sing Navy songs. Still no Jen. About one hour went by and I started to lose hope. Then Jen came back into the room escorted by JG.

"You ok?"

Jen sat next to me and began to cry.

"What's up?"

"I have been ordered to stay away from you because of the hospital policy on fraternizing with patients."

"Uh, excuse me? I won't be a patient here much longer. I am going to NIH." I put my arm around Jen.

"It doesn't matter. I was informed that my duty schedule would be changed in order to keep us apart. And that if I really love you I should let you go."

"This is bullshit. Did she threaten you?"

"JG said if I continued to see you that I'd be violating a lawful order in regards to your well being."

"My well being includes good morale!" I started to get up. "What the fuck!"

"It's because you need down time and you refuse to take it. I'm sorry Jay." Jen kissed my cheek and walked out of the room. Walked right out of my life. I didn't see her again. It was all bullshit.

JG came in shortly afterwards. "I'm sorry. But you are about to go through a protocol that has a high mortality rate. You need to think about her."

"I am. I am thinking about having some fucking happiness while I do this shit. If it wasn't for the Navy I wouldn't have cancer in the first fucking place."

"Is it fair to put her through all this and then die? Because it could happen and you could ruin her." JG got in my face.

"She was willing. Isn't that good enough?"

"No, it's not. She doesn't know any better. I'm trying to save her the heartache."

"Oh, so you think I'll die, too, huh? What the fuck ever Ma'am!" I stood up and started packing my belongings. "I guess I will just die alone then. It's nice to know that I don't deserve to be happy."

"It's not that. If you make it, then by all means, try again. But right now you need to focus on your treatments. The decisions you are making with her are unethical. It's going to get you killed."

"I'm glad you are looking out for me. I'll remember that when I write my book about this whole experience." But I knew she was right. I knew that taking Jen into this hell would have been wrong. I know that now. I know because I saw what it did to Leanna. JG was right. I was wrong. But at the time I felt like I was right. There went another love out the door. All compliments of cancer.

***

My return to Maine left me with nothing but anger. As soon as I got home I took the Jeep and went to the Maine Mall. It was time to get things off my mind. It was time to see Leanna. The mall was packed as usual. Teens running around acting like they are some type of gods, not knowing how horrible the real world is. They were living in a dream world. I made my way to Leanna's workplace. There was a line so I waited by the eyeglass store. I wasn't paying much attention to the world around me. Then, without warning I felt a sharp pain in my side "Hey, Jay!"

I'm not sure who the girl was who poked me in my ribs but she ended up putting her thumb in between my ribcage via the hole from my chest tube. I do remember she was short, blond, cute and feisty. Her thumb was lodged in my rib. I dropped to the floor in pain and she went with me. I will call her 'the assassin' because she could have killed me.

"FUCK!" People looked my way. I pulled the assassin's thumb from my ribs and quickly grabbed some napkins to use as a quick fix as blood began to fill my shirt.

"Oh, Jesus! I'm so sorry Jay!"

"It's ok." I stood up, waved like I was a celebrity and winked at Leanna and Jess, who were both leaning over the counter. "It's all right everyone, carry on." The assassin apologized a few dozen more times and I helped her regain composure. "Well, I didn't expect that to happen. Are you an assassin or what?"

"I'm really sorry, Jay. I didn't know."

"Of course you did. Who paid you to try and kill me? Hmm? Who?" I got her feeling really guilty. It wasn't a big deal. These things happen.

"Welcome home, Jay." Jess waved.

"Hey there." Leanna came out from behind the counter and gave me a hug. It felt weird. Of all the people I knew, Leanna seemed the happiest to see me.

"What's up kiddo?" I pulled her ball cap over her eyes.

"Not much. I wrote you some notes." Leanna dug through her pockets and pulled out a handful of papers. They were neatly folded into a squares.

"Thank you." Leanna went back to work as people started lining up again. I sat down and unfolded each note carefully. The contents mostly talked about how boring school was and how much she missed me. It was cute. Flattering, actually. The assassin sat next to me and continued to apologize. I blocked her out and just inhaled the smell of the food court. It was Maine. I was home.

I went into the Dream Machine, the mall arcade and played House of the Dead. I loved gun games. They kept me up on my target practice. One shot, one kill, if you hit the video game zombies in the head. I did this for a few hours until Leanna got off from work. I watched her try and sneak up on me but her reflection on the video game screen gave her away.

"Hey, Leanna. Thank you for the notes."

"How do you do that?"

"I'm in the Navy. Pay attention to detail kiddo."

"I wish you'd stop calling me kiddo. You sound like you're my dad."

"Don't go there. I already feel a bit funny about hanging with you." I turned around after I cleared the stage. "But you're just so cute." I pinched her cheek and twisted it.

"Thanks. So what are we going to do?"

"How about a movie? Let's hit the Maine Mall Cinema."

"Awesome!" Leanna gave me a hug and watched me play for a while longer.

"First we need grub. Let's go to Chili's." Chili's was a unique place for me. In Texas, one of my shipmates Ken and I went to the opening of the first Chili's in Corpus Christi. I made it my religious duty to go there all the time. It was where I told my closest circle of friends about cancer. It was where Trevor cried when he heard the news. It was a safe place for me. Best of all, they served great margaritas.

At dinner Leanna and I talked about life. I kept Jen out of the conversation. We spoke mostly about Leanna and school, though, I don't think she was a big fan of education. She was more into softball. Leanna was quite the catcher. She also liked to brag about all the fucked up shit she used to do. Her ex. The abuse. Getting her nose broken with a pipe. Her use of drugs, alcohol and her smoking. I wasn't a fan of any of this. But I felt like a hypocrite telling her that drinking was bad as I pounded down a margarita.

"You know, half that shit isn't cool." I scolded her.

"Yes it is. Half the sports teams in South Portland do drugs and drink. I'm just fitting in."

"Why doesn't anyone do anything about it?"

"Because what would happen if the star athletes got busted? They do get caught, but the sports directors cover it up." That really pissed me off. I wasn't a fan of jocks and this shit just confirmed why.

"Cute. I ought to bust them."

"It's easy enough. Tonight there is a party at one of the coach's houses. I know there is pot there."

"Just thinking about it is blowing my buzz. Next topic." I finished my drink and ordered another.

"Another? You're going to get drunk. Who's going to drive?"

"The movie theatre is next door. We can drive over." I was pretty much gone. My fingers and face were totally numb. I had no feeling in my tongue. I felt pretty fucked up. Yet, despite all my preaching about bad behavior, I was going to drive drunk. It wasn't too hard. There was very little traffic, and when I focused after drinking that much I could function.

When we got to the parking lot I looked around. Leanna was standing next to me holding my arm. "Which movie shall we see?" I asked and Leanna stood on her toes and kissed me. I looked at her. Those eyes, that expression. I had lost Dawn and Jen. I put my hands on her face and felt her skin for a second. It was soft, but solid. Her blond hair blew to one side as the wind rushed by from the open landscape of the Maine Turnpike. "I love you," I said.

There was a long pause as Leanna's eyes teared up. She hugged me and then kissed my lips. I don't know why I said it. It was wrong. But I had said it. Why? Because here was someone who would love me no matter how sick I might become. She would be my best friend and she would humor my stupid whims. At that moment Leanna became more than just the girl I picked up at the mall. She became an essential part of my life.

"Yo, Libby!" A shout broke the silence. I looked around and ducked behind some nearby cars.

"Who the fuck?"

"Who was that?" Leanna ducked with me.

"I don't know. Sniper?" I was drunk. I put on my game face and got ready to take incoming fire. I scoped out the windows of the Days Inn. Nothing. I looked toward the I-Hop. Nothing. I stood up and peeked at the cars. I couldn't see anyone.

"Sniper? Funny." Leanna stood up and dragged me across the parking lot.

"Libby!" I heard the shout again. This time in front of me. It was Sturdavant, or Stu, for short. One of my shipmates from the Reserve Center and a friend. He was in his pimp-mobile with a gal. Stu was the Brotha alright.

"Fuck, dude. I thought you were a sniper."

"Damn, Libby, are you drunk?"

"Umm." I looked side to side in a devious way. "Yep."

"Do you need a ride home?"

"Nope, I've got him Stu." Leanna pulled me along and smiled.

"Stay out of trouble, Lib!" Stu shouted as we made our way to the concrete steps.

"Never!" I bounced off one of the movie poster display cases.

"Sweet." I smiled and pulled Leanna close to me as we walked up to pay for the movie. Again, another escape.

***

Returning to Bethesda this time wasn't as easy as before. There was no plane, no solo travel, no control. My parents escorted me via car all the way there. Instead of going to the Naval Hospital we headed to the National Institute of Health. The place that would be my home of sorts away from home. Imagine, if you will, a city within a city. Not some fancy West Coast mall or some New York subway shopping extravaganza, but a real city within a city. NIH was a city within a city. Before I could start the EPOCH II study I had to meet with Doctor Wilson and his staff. I also had to go through tons of tests. I found myself at awe over the whole NIH campus. In order to enter you have to pass through one of several gates guarded by a security force that might have been made up of professional mercenaries. When you drive down Route 335 the Bethesda Naval Hospital sits on one side and NIH on the other. The Navy hospital is big, the view of NIH is blocked by trees. You almost don't know it's there because METRO has a station in front of it. Just past the METRO station is the gate. As you pull into NIH you turn right and head towards the main building. That's when you get the shock. Dozens of very tall buildings fill the sky. It's uncanny. After a lot of driving we finally found the parking garage. Then we walked what seemed like a gazillion steps to get to the Outpatient Clinic. First I went to a lab where I was stuck by the best of the best. Professional phlebotomists. No double sticks and butterfly needles! A butterfly is this little needle that can be plugged into a vacu-tube. It does less damage and is easier to stick into someone with shitty veins. I remember signing in and waiting in an open room where fish tanks surrounded us. There was some soft elevator music playing over the NIH speakers. A phlebotomist called my name and I went into a room full of cubicles. I was slightly nervous. I saw the vacu-tubes in a box and started to shiver. The woman, a black lady who was so beautiful I had to keep myself from hitting on her, had me sit next to her. She asked to see the patient band that was provided to me at the registration desk ten yards away.

"Please don't stick me in my hand. See my Bermuda Triangle?" I flipped my hand over to show her a triangle formed by scars from bad sticks.

"Sweety, just slap your arm down and let me handle it." She pulled me close, holding my wrist in her hand. The rubber gloves she wore had me wonder if she'd be able to feel a vein. She gave me a stress ball, smiled and put a tourniquet around my left arm. "Squeeze it." She winked. I began to pump that poor red stress ball with all my might. "Ok, you're going to feel a stick."

When I get stuck I usually bite my index finger until it turns purple. It's not because I can't handle the stress of getting stuck, but it takes away from the focus of that small prick. But before I could even get my finger in my mouth I was already stuck and blood was pumping into the butterfly line and into the vacu-tube.

"Holy shit!"

"What? Did that hurt?"

"No, that's why I am amazed. What did you use?"

"It's called a butterfly. It doesn't scar the veins up and makes it easier on patients."

"Oh man. I want that for now on!"

"Well NIH exclusively uses them."

That was a good start to my experience at NIH. People who actually wanted to put you through less pain. After the lab I went for vitals. Blood pressure, pulse, and the other basics. That clears me for the next part. Testing. You see, NIH is all about the research. They want to know everything about your body, right up to that annoying twitch in your left cheek. It's important.

My next stop was to get an injection of radioactive material called gallium. What it does is settle into the areas where there might be active cancer. The nurse sat me down and brought in a tray with a large piece of lead. Inside the lead was a syringe with the material inside it. Like the phlebotomist, the nurse offered me all the sorts of comforts as she stuck me. Two sticks in one day. Not cool. After that I had to drink contrast for a CAT Scan. Contrast helps expand certain passages in the body. The contrast that NIH used had Crystal Lite in it. Great stuff. I could sit there and chug that stuff like it was going out of style. And I did. Other patients would gag it down. Meanwhile I was playing drinking games with mine. Every time the fish in the fish tank looked at me (NIH had them everywhere) I'd take a ten second chug. It was amusing. After five minutes or so I finished one whole jug, so the nurse handed me another.

"I'll make you keep drinking them for a half hour." The lady at the desk informed me. "So slow down."

I smirked, popped the lid "Bottoms down, booties up." I chugged the whole thing right in front of her. The whole damn thing. Then like a pro I slammed down the empty container on the desk and smiled. Those damn things just kept coming. I wasn't aware of how badly I'd be paying for it later. A half hour later it was my turn. I went into the CT room and laid down on a hard white table that fed into the machine. Another nurse started an IV for the dye used during the procedure. The dye helps define the body and adds great detail to the scan.

"Now it might give you a warm feeling once it starts going in. The scan will take about thirty to forty minutes. If you need to go to the bathroom do it now."

My bladder was fine. But she was right. An automated voice warned me that the injection was going in. The CT dye warmed me up quickly. Especially in my groin. It felt pretty strange, but what the hell, I might as well enjoy it. I closed my eyes and followed the instructions: Take a deep breath, hold it, breath. I think the voice repeated it about ten times before I started to doze off. In my mind I tried to focus on something less stressful. Cable, the character from Marvel Comics kept popping into my mind. I have no clue why. The last thing I read about him was that he and his alternate reality counterpart Stryfe, were duking it out on the moon. It made no sense. Still, his armor looked cool. Maybe that's what it was. I was always a sucker for steel armor. When the scan finished the nurse came in and sat me up slowly.

"You might want to take it easy there. Especially if this is your first time."

"Sounds erotic." I smiled and stood up fast. Damn did that room spin! Really, when a nurse says to take it slow, do it. "Am I all set?"

"Yep, we'll get the scans up to your doctors today. They should be there by the time you reach your appointment."

"Nice." I went into the bathroom with a serious need to fart. Yes fart. It was from drinking all that contrast. I sat down on the toilet and tried to let it out quietly. No such luck. Not only did I let out the biggest gas exchange in the history of humankind. It was so loud it almost blew me off the seat. But the contrast I'd drunk came blasting out for about three minutes. For three entire minutes my intestines let go of everything I'd had that day. Of course that would be four jugs of contrast. It hurt. I am lucky I didn't rupture my stomach or tear my ass open. When I came out of the bathroom I was blushing. I tried to act cool, but everyone had heard it. One little girl came up to me and asked if I was ok. My parents laughed and the rest of the people who were sitting there joined in.

"Well I have to say, I feel much better."

"Sounds like you do." My dad laughed.

That afternoon my parents and I had lunch at the NIH cafeteria. It was pretty cool. Not like the Navy Hospital. They had foods from all over the world. You couldn't go wrong. I wasn't too hungry since I was still having stomach issues. I was nervous. My mother and father kept talking about the hospital, almost drooling. It was impressive. It was the one place where the best people in medicine worked. My parents must have felt special. They were. They took time out of their lives to drive me down here for all the testing.

"How do you feel, guy?" My mother asked.

"I'm nervous. That 80% mortality rate is bothering me. I guess I'll live fast and die young."

"Don't worry about it. The people here are the best in their fields." My dad tried to reassure me. It wasn't helping.

The trip in the elevator to the Oncology floor was a long one. The door opened to a bank of windows displaying all of Bethesda. In the distance I saw towers and the Mormon church. The Mormon church looked like the Castle of Lions from the cartoon Voltron. At night it illuminated the skyline. Today it blended in with the rest of the scenery. To the left of us was the door to the Out Patient Oncology Offices. We walked through it to find dozens of cancer patients, all very sick and all looking like they were on their last leg. I realized this was the end for me. Soon I would be one of them. My parents escorted me to the front desk where I gave my name and appointment time. I was instructed to sit and wait.

"Jason Libby." A woman came out from one of the rooms to the left of the front desk. She was an elderly black woman who had the sweetest face. "Let me be the first to welcome you to NIH." She shook my hand and took me over to a set of medical scales. I emptied my pockets and stepped up. "Are you scared?"

"Should I be?"

"Everyone is at first, Jason." She touched my arm and motioned me to step down. "But you'll get used to it. There are a lot of nice people here."

"I can tell." I pointed my thumb over my shoulder to the mass of cancer patients in the waiting room.

"You look worse before you get better." I wish I could remember her name. It would do her justice. Because she was right. It does take looking worse in order to get better. She took my vitals and sent me back to the waiting room.

I watched everyone and wanted to leave. Yet I knew I couldn't. I was there because I chose to be. If I tried to back out now the Navy would catch up to me. By the time it was my turn to meet with the Nurse Practitioner, Karen, I was ready to hear my fate. My parents and I were taken into a room where we met with my first NIH doctor. As we walked into the room a Pakistani doctor who had taken care of me and the same one I had hit at the Naval Hospital passed by.

"Mr. Libby," he said in his broken English, "it's good to see you again."

"Um, yeah." I walked into the room fired up. I didn't want him touching me ever again. That is when I met nurse Karen.

"I will be working your case for the next six months." she said as she started giving me the scoop about EPOCH II and what NIH expected of me. She was short with long black hair, and judging from her accent must have been from South America. She was very likable. With her was another nurse. I don't remember her name, but I do remember her being a bitch. It was she whom I talked to on the phone about the EPOCH II study. She had been pushy with me and acted like I deserved to have cancer. When I posed questions she came back at me with an attitude. But Karen wasn't like that at all.

She told me I would be reporting to the cardiac unit for the insertion of a central line. This would go near my heart so I would need to be monitored. They would put it in while I was awake. That was not sounding fun. Then Karen said I would report to the outpatient clinic to get an IV pump and my chemo drugs. I would return daily to NIH for a new bag of drugs. This meant staying at the hotel on base across the street. It also meant spending a whole week with my mother, who volunteered to come with me. Joy. After that I could return home for three weeks. During that time I would inject myself with Neupogen daily in the fat of my stomach until my counts returned to normal. Which also meant having daily blood draws.

After that treatment Karen explained that I would report to the inpatient unit where I would receive the first lethal dose of EPOCH II. I would have to stay in the hospital for at least three days because the dose was going to be enough to kill a human and they wanted me to be monitored closely. If I survived, I would go home for three more weeks. Again, I would get my blood count checked every day and shoot up with Neupogen. This whole cycle would repeat itself for 6 months. If I survived there was no guarantee that I'd be cured. I'd need to continue follow-ups for five whole years. Even then I would only be given a tentative cured status. Talk about nothing to look forward to.

Once Karen finished explaining all this Doctor Wilson came in. He offered a quick hello. He was nice enough, I guess, but he was intimidating. It was his study, his baby. The last thing he wanted to deal with was some cocky sailor. But he got me, ego and all.

"I read your last chemo reports. Your body actually built a resistance to the CHOP therapy. It won't happen this time."

"No problem, Doc. I can take anything you throw at me."

"Good, because this isn't a game. Take it seriously and you might live."

"I'm Jay. I don't die. Didn't you read the memo?"

Doctor Wilson shook his head and asked my parents if they had any questions. They talked for a while as I gazed out the window. It reminded me of something out of Star Wars. A vast green landscape, ripe for the plundering. When everyone finished talking Doctor Wilson looked at me. "You have one more test. A double bone marrow biopsy. Then you may return home for a few days until we get the test results back."

The sound of a double bone marrow biopsy intrigued me. I wondered what that meant. I ended up at the outpatient clinic where I met some more oncology nurses. I was put into a room and asked to gown up. After that I was placed face down on a table and informed I would receive some injections for the pain. Those hurt as much as the actual biopsy. The nurse jammed a large needle into my hip on both sides and injected anesthesia to numb the spots. After that she placed a tray with a monster needle next to me. I almost panicked. I was assured I wouldn't feel a thing. But I did. I heard it in my ears. The grinding of bone as they burrowed into my hips to retrieve two bone marrow samples. It hurt so fucking bad I wanted to belt someone. I was certain that the anesthesia hadn't kicked in yet. God knows I didn't tell them. When that was finished one nurse patted me on the ass and told me I did great. All I could do was smile.

***

The next day I had to return for a Gallium scan. It was a long process in which I had to lay on my back with my arms above my head. I couldn't move for about three hours. Nor could I pee. When we arrived I was nervous. The room where the machine was had dim lights. I imagine to help you relax. The only bright light was emanating from the computer screens and buttons. It was like walking into a science fiction movie. I half expected some chick with pointy ears to step out and offer me some fucked up hand that looked like a cross between a flipper and some European sex toy. Instead I got an old lady who looked like she had been battle scarred from years of exposure to radiation. I laid down on the bench and put my hands above my head. It was like being on the rack. No whips, no chains, just three hours of boring buzzing. Oh joy. I kept falling asleep. Once in a while I'd snap to after letting out a loud snore. My eyes would catch the light in the room and then I'd go back to sleep.

When I awoke I couldn't feel my hands. They were completely asleep. I was instructed to lower my arms, but they weren't going anywhere. It reminded me of the film *PCU*, when the chap watching TV through the entire film gets up to change a fuse and screams "Pins and needles, pins and needles!" as he collapses in pain. Once the numbness went away, those damn pins and needles kicked in. I smacked my dead hands together attempting to restore order to the machine known as Jay. "Come on bitch, stop tingling."

"Excuse me?" The nurse looked at me like I was some barbarian.

"My hands, I can't feel them. Bloody hell!" I smacked my arms on the bench until I started to feel semi normal. Once restored, I was able to move my fingers. They were all ghost white. There hadn't been blood in them for a while. My feet were fine. I could stand like any other person, but my arms kinda hung there. The only good motion that I could manage was swinging them like a monkey. At least I could move my fingers. "Well that was just peachy. Time to get the hell out of here and go home."

***

The news from the Navy was that I needed to move into the outpatient barracks. I was smart about it this time. Before I even left I made sure I had a room. A private room. Since my last stay, the old barracks had been closed and a new one built. This one was fancy and really had a better feel to it. The walls were brand new, white, and the place looked like a hotel. My preparation for moving down to Bethesda was pretty simple. I planned to pack up my new car and drive there. Of course I had to tell Leanna, but as if it mattered. It was best that I leave her.

"So do you really have to move?"

"Yeah, I do. Sorry kiddo. But it has been fun."

"Will you at least write to me?"

"Sure I will. Got your address in my little black book." Over the last two years I had accumulated over twenty names and numbers of girls. Most from Philadelphia, but some from Texas and here in Maine. The ones with stars represented how many times I'd slept with them. It was pretty pathetic to keep count, but at the time I was ego driven.

"I see, along with how many other girls?"

"Don't worry. Not like I'll have time for anything else."

I was right. There wasn't time for anything else. My car was filled with a footlocker, a TV and two large duffel bags. Picture it, I was driving a Mazda MX-3, a little red Jap-mobile that was meant for picking up chicks not big moves. I barely had room for the little cooler packed with my beverages. I didn't go to see Leanna before I left. Our conversation was strictly by phone. I didn't want to make the move any harder than it already was.

The whole way to Bethesda I listened to Manowar and a selection of music that inspired me to drive. A lot of things went through my mind. Here I was driving myself to my impending doom. I was alone. I would remain alone, unless Jen disobeyed orders. It was a shitty deal. Who would take care of me when I was too sick to leave my room? I started to miss my friends very quickly. It's a long drive when you know where you're going and it's not good.

When I arrived at the Naval Hospital Barracks I was met with some bad news. "We're sorry. Your room was given to someone else. You'll have to stay in our temporary housing until we can get you set up."

"Temporary housing?" I was pissed.

"Yes, that room over there. You'll have about three roommates."

"What the fuck?" I pulled out my orders and slammed them down in front of the very small black sailor sitting in front of me. "You see this?! Specific orders for a private room because of the chemo I am having."

"I understand, but I have never seen these before. So unless your command sends me a new copy I cannot give you a private room."

"Fine, I'll have them faxed."

"That won't be good enough. They need to be mailed."

"Excuse me? I'm about ready to kick your ass. This is insane."

"Yelling at me won't get you very far. I'll call your command on Monday and get this straightened out."

"It's fucking Friday you asshole!" By this point I had drawn the attention of a few of my shipmates who were watching TV in the lounge. A couple of them got up and walked over.

"What's the problem?" one sailor asked.

"He says he has orders, but I haven't seen any." The guy behind the desk responded.

"This is Libby, I got his paperwork. Why isn't his room ready?"

"We had to place someone else in it with higher priority." This meant that he gave the room to one of his buddies. It always happens. The ole' "hook me up, brotha" routine.

"Look, the kid has orders. I suggest you clear out the occupant of that room."

"But I can't."

"I guess you didn't see the red flag on the paperwork." The red flag. It meant that I had been involved in Senatorial business. In this case, I blew the whistle on the Naval Hospital on their treatment of cancer patients. Senator Snowe was more than willing to look into my allegations. All of which were true.

"It'll take a few hours."

"Do it then!"

Apparently the sailor who had stepped in was in charge of the barracks. I thanked him and went to the phone and called NIH. I was almost in tears. Here I was about to die and I was going to be going through the same shit I went through last time.

The nurse who answered the phone couldn't understand why I had moved. "You know NIH pays to fly you back and forth, right?"

"They do?" I dropped to my knees in tears.

"Yes, and we will provide you with a voucher to stay at a local hotel."

"So I can go home?" I whimpered.

"There is no need for you to stay down here. If you can receive in patient care in Maine, go home. You should be with family during your treatments."

I lost it. Tears poured down my face and I curled up on the floor by the phone. The sailor who had been in charge came over. "You ok?"

"They said I can go home and NIH will pay for my travel expenses."

"Great news. If you want you can pull up a cot and take a nap before you go back."

"Will the Navy cover my hospital stays in Maine?"

"They should. NIH is paying for your treatments. Here is the number you need to call to make sure you are all set." He handed me a piece of paper with the phone number to one of the hospital administrators who specialized in these special circumstances.

"Thank you." I stood up and regained my composure. I marched over to the billing officer and requested to speak to a counselor. The conversation was quick.

"Yes, we'll pay all hospital bills if NIH is paying for your primary treatment and meds."

It was like a massive weight had been lifted off of me. The one thing that burned in my mind: home. There would be no nap. I was going to power drive my ass back to Maine and sleep in my bed. I had arrived in Bethesda at about noon and I left at 4pm. Before I hit the road I returned to the outpatient barracks. "I don't need a room! I am going back to Maine."

"You really should at least rest a little." The guy behind the desk suggested.

"No offense, but fuck you. I am outta here!" I gave him the finger and returned to my car, which had enjoyed the short rest. I rolled off hospital property with the song *Hail and Kill* blasting, windows down.

***

The human body is good at withstanding sleep deprivation. As a sailor I learned the value of a few hours rest here and there in order to maintain peak performance. My drive to DC had been fully energized with no feeling of sleepiness. The return home was different. I used to call it driving subconsciously. I could drive practically sleeping with my eyes open. If my body felt something wrong it'd wake me up to react. In this state, I could get a good amount of rest but I would see things, talk to people who weren't there and generally act pretty fucked up. I hadn't taken into account all the energy I had spent during that day. The mental strain of not having a room was a lot more traumatizing than you might think.

When I reached Rhode Island I was totally gone. Asleep at the wheel, having a conversation with someone who wasn't really there. Everything seemed ok. I was on the road, but the imaginary person next to me kept telling me to pull into the next rest stop. "Come on Jay, there is nothing to prove by going on. The rest stop is a few miles ahead. Take a quick two hour nap."

"I can do it. I want to be in my bed."

"Jay, you are almost completely asleep at the wheel."

"I can do it, just keep me talking."

"I can't, look at me!"

I glanced over and the phantom waved, I looked back to the road and there he was, sitting on the hood. "Hey, get off the hood!"

"I'm not on the hood, I'm sitting right here." He was back sitting in the passenger seat.

"Shit, you're right. I need the sleep." I pulled into the rest stop at about 90mph, slid into a parking spot and locked my doors. I slipped the handy knife I kept in my glove box under my shirt and closed my eyes.

"Goodnight, Jay."

"Goodnight."

About two hours went by before the sun's glare pierced my eyelids. Daybreak. I opened my eyes knowing that I had to hit the road. I was well rested. There was no sign of my copilot. Instead I watched as a family evacuated from their mini-van and ran for the restrooms. I sat my seat up and put the knife away. When my car door opened the silence ended. The sound of trucks roaring up the highway brought me back to reality for sure. I stretched toward the sky, reaching for the heavens. My back cracked. "FUUUCK! Time to get rolling." The restroom was far from clean. Urine on the floors with toilet paper soaking some of it up. The smell of piss broke through my morning nose clog.   The   radio programming on the way home was great. I hit one of the shock jock stations and listened as two men talked about why they hate kids. "Doesn't it drive you nuts when you are out to eat and some little nose picker keeps staring at you?" I laughed. "And then there are those mothers who think you really give a shit about their kids and make you sit there while they show you photos. Seriously lady, I don't give a BEEP!"

These guys were right. I wasn't a fan of kids. They were always loud, annoying and half the time so were their parents. When I am out to eat I don't want to hear kids.

"It's like, I have this date and my girl is busy laughing at the nose picker behind me. I don't want her getting any ideas. I want to take her home afterwards and get laid, not have a family." These guys were reading my mind. "Then there are these women who just keep pumping out kids. They live off of welfare and keep having kids. I think we should just tie them off after one kid."

I knew women like that. They were single moms who plotted how to live off the S,tate. That still pisses me off today. Get a fucking job or find someone who is responsible enough to date. Half these women think that bar flies and hicks are the best thing in the world. Sorry, doesn't work that way. Most beer chuggers are useless. They'll spend your welfare check faster than you can, all on beer. The radio show made me forget about my problems. By the time I hit Maine I was grateful to be sterile.

***

While I wanted to celebrate being home, it was a short stay. My mother decided she would travel with me to DC in order to make sure I behaved and followed medical advice. To be honest, the thought of traveling alone bothered me, so while I didn't want her company it was better than nothing. There is a lot to be said about a mother and son who hate each other sitting together on a plane. Then again maybe not. There is nothing noteworthy about it. You sit there and humor one another until you can get off the plane. What really made the trip interesting was having to share a hotel room at the Navy Lodge. I'm a guy who has guy issues, like farting. When you have to do it you have to do it. After having chemo it became painful to not fart, and I mean crippling. Weird side effect with no scientific value. So every time I needed to fart I'd have to go into the bathroom or outside. That lasted about fifteen minutes.

After we arrived in Bethesda we took a taxi to the Navy Lodge, signed in and then went to NIH. It was the same routine. Vitals, blood work, CT, and a visit to the outpatient clinic. What was different this time was the twenty minutes I spent in the intensive care unit getting a central line. This handy, LARGE IV line goes into your neck. It has a few ports to allow for many different meds to be pumped into you. At first I didn't think too highly of it, but as I got used to the ports, the central line became my new best friend. The ICU itself was pretty cool. It looked like something out of Star Trek. A circled unit with beds around the nursing station, there were monitors everywhere and lots of lights. Each patient area had a glass door except for mine. That was because I was just there to get the central line. Why ICU? Because the central line goes into your aorta. One slip and you could find yourself up shit creek without a paddle. I went into ICU alone. Walking through the halls of NIH was like walking through a time warp. I was surrounded by nice new walls, then old brick, then white futuristic walls. By the time I arrived I felt disoriented.

"Is this where I go for my central line?"

"Your name?" a nurse sitting at the desk inquired. The nursing staff at NIH dressed in their own fashion. I noticed that only the lab rats actually dressed in a specific uniform. She was blond, thin, probably in her late thirties, but darn cute.

"Libby, Jason."

"Oh, yes. We've been waiting for you!" She seemed really excited. Probably because she was the nurse doing the procedure.

"Is that good or bad?"

"That's great. It's always exciting to meet people from studies. You are doing a great thing. If the study works then you could be responsible for saving lives." Back then that made me feel special. Now I find it slightly unnerving.

"Yeah, well I didn't have a choice. The Navy required me to receive treatment. I'm lucky they let me pick."

"You're in the Navy too? That's great!" Ok, Tony the Tiger was worrying me. She escorted me to a bed and instructed me to remove my shirt. I sat on the cozy bed where the nurse began to place all these sticky things on me for an EKG. Another nurse brought in a tray of needles, a suture kit, a package with that monster central line and some medication (which turned out to be anesthesia).

"What we are going to do is numb the area. Then we will begin the procedure. You'll be awake through the whole thing. So just breathe when we tell you to and it'll all work just fine. Oh yeah, don't move either." If you could have seen the needles they were using you would have run in terror.

The first needle was used to numb the spot where the line would go in. I heard a popping sound as the needle penetrated. I felt it too, but it was the sound that bothered me. Sometime take a piece of rubber and stretch it to the max. Then take an awl and puncture it. That was the sound I heard in my inner ear. I clenched my fist and let a single tear drop down my face.

"How are you doing?"

"Um, you have a bloody huge needle in my neck. How do you think I'm doing?"

"We'll need to let the anesthesia kick in then we will add more." The nurse poked the side of my neck where they had been prodding. It wasn't even close to numb. A few minutes later the nurse returned. Still poking, they stuck another needle in my neck.

"This sucks. I have to do this every other cycle?"

"According to protocol, yes."

I chuckled as she poked me once again. This time I was pretty numb. "Ok, now it's slightly kicking in."

"Just slightly?"

"Well, just to give you a heads up on how my body works, here's the scoop. My body completely fought off the chemo drugs from my CHOP. I didn't even go neutropenic."

"Are you serious? That is amazing."

Maybe she didn't take me seriously or maybe she did. That bit of information is hard to take in. Yet it did happen, so what could I do? Nothing. I sat there while she continued to stick me with that stupid needle.

After about thirty minutes of getting stuck, poked and agitated they were ready to insert my central line. I was instructed to lie back on the bed and the nurses tilted the bed so my feet were up and my head was facing down at an angle. Another woman came in dressed like a surgeon. "Careful, this one is a wise guy." My nurse warned.

"Italian or Russian?"

"Scottish." I replied as she started to work without much warning.

"Ok, you will feel pressure in your neck. That will be the line.

Would you like to watch?" The doctor handed my nurse a mirror.

"Sure, why the heck not?" Believe it or not, I watched a little. I was intrigued by the whole procedure. First they ran a metal sheath into my neck and down into the aorta. The main part of the central line was inside the sheath, much like a tampon dispenser. Once the metal part reached its destination the doctor pulled it out and the plastic line was left in. From here the nurses placed the caps on the ends of the individual exterior ports.

"Make sure that you tell us if you feel anything unusual in your chest. Like a flutter."

"Sure."

I watched as the doctor slid that monster sheath into my neck. All I felt was insane pressure, as if someone were poking me in the neck with a stick. I felt a little flutter, but it was nothing to freak out about. If you think about it, your body is bound to react when a strange object is inserted into your neck. I braved it out and watched. Once the sheath was in, they slid it out, and began stitching the remaining line to my neck. I hate stitches. I really do. I felt those. Lucky for me it took only about four stitches before I was done. Next they flushed each line. If you have never experienced a saline flush consider yourself lucky. It left a crappy taste in my nose. Yes, a taste in my nose.

"Well that went nice and smooth, Mr. Libby. You now have your first central line."

I clapped my hands and smiled. "Do I get a prize?"

"Yes, you can report to the outpatient clinic for your chemo bags and pump."

"Ah, yes." And so it began.

***

The first round of chemo consisted of carrying an IV pump and bag around with me for about four days. Each day I was required to swap them out for new ones at the outpatient clinic. I was no novice when it came to IV pumps. In high school I had worked for New England Life Care delivering medical supplies and pumps. I'd learned the ins and outs of IV therapy. Patrick, my boss, taught me well. I could turn a pump on, insert the lines, and program them. So when the nurse in the outpatient clinic handed me my first pump and tried to offer instruction I just slapped the chemo bag into the shoulder case they gave me, placed the line in the pump and switched it on. I wanted to say I was a true pro, but I wasn't. I was the patient.

"Yeah, I got it. No need for the long lecture."

"Jason, cooperate." My mother scolded me. She did that quite frequently; loved to belittle me in front of people.

"Hey, I know what the hell I am doing."

"No you don't. Just listen." My mother looked to the nurse. "He is such a pain in the ass."

This wasn't really unusual. My mother and I fought constantly. If we got along there was something wrong. I hated my mother because she always blamed me for her misery. When I was a child she would yell at me for the dumbest things. My room wasn't clean, I was lazy, I watched too much TV, I was in the way. When her carton of cigarettes vanished I was to blame. My mother wasn't well. When she tried to commit suicide she blamed everyone but herself. All of a sudden my grandparents and I needed therapy. It was insane. She loved me through hate. She took out her shitty situations on me. Instead of rebelling like most kids did, I stayed true to my passions, playing RPGs like Marvel Superheroes™ and Heroes Unlimited™. I used my friends as shields against her. As long as my friends were around she was semi pleasant to me. I know she couldn't help herself. Look at the environment she was in. My stepfather was cheating on her, my grandmother was a demanding beast who was self centered. She ran my mother through the grinder. My grandfather loved my mother, but after he died she went and read his diaries. In a passage about my mother's adoption he'd written "We're disappointed that it's a girl." When I was born he wrote a line that went something like: "I finally have the boy I always wanted." It explained why my grandfather favored me above everyone. It also meant I had a lot to live up to. But my mother didn't take it too well. It made her even more viscous than before. I would have felt the same way I suppose. Maybe she already knew about my grandfather's feelings. That could explain why she was the way she was. Then again, my grandparents did a lot for her. Sending her to school, taking her on trips around the world, and other really cultured activities.

When the pump started I remember saying to myself "This is the end." Slowly I began to taste the drugs on my tongue and in my nose. It was apparent that I was going to once again lose all sense of taste. My taste buds screamed one last breath and died. My mother and I walked back to the Navy Lodge where I dropped down on the nice hotel bed and put my feet up.

"I need a nap and then we can go get a bite to eat." My mother collapsed on her bed and rested her head on her pillow. I could only imagine the pain she was suffering. I see mothers every day at my job at the hospital, emotionally tormented by the loss of their children, and I understood why my mother was always exhausted after a simple walk across the street.

I grabbed my calling card and picked up the phone. It was time to dial Leanna and let her know how I was doing. In all this mess she was still there for me: this teenage girl with no real concept of how bad it really was. The phone rang twice and Brenda picked up. "Hey this is Jay, is Leanna home?"

"Yep, one second Jay."

I waited anxiously. I wanted to hear her voice. I needed to hear her voice. It offered some escape from my hell.

"Hey, Jay!" Her bubbly voice traveled through my ears and sunk into my heart.

"Hey, kiddo. Have a good day at school?"

"Yeah, got softball later. Do you plan on catching one of my games when you get home?"

"Sure. Not like I can do anything."

"How did your treatment go?"

"Well, I am now bagged and tagged. Got an IV pump stuck to me for a few days."

"Wow, does it hurt?"

"I'm Jay, do you think it hurts?"

"Well, does it?"

"Girl, I am like God. I can handle anything." The God complex. I used it to cover my low self-esteem. I still do to this day. Part of it has become reality. My military training made me blind to a lot of dangers. Still, I was vulnerable. Leanna was my weak spot.

"Ok, God. Well I need to run. Call me tonight?"

"Ok. Sounds like a plan."

When I hung up the phone my mother opened her eyes and looked at me. "I don't know what you see in that girl."

"I see a person who wants to be there."

"I see you going to jail."

"I'm not fucking her. We just hang out. At this point I need it." I did need it. I needed Leanna. She was quickly becoming my best friend.

"Whatever."

My mother reached for the remote and I swiped it. Channel surfing led me to a cartoon that would become my all time favorite, *The Tick*. This was the first time I had seen it. I remember as a kid collecting the comics and reading about it in a magazine. The cartoon is about this super strong, super indestructible blue costumed superhero whose sidekick is Arthur, an accountant who dresses like a moth. It is satire at its best. The Tick's battle cry was "Spoon" while Arthur kept saying "Not in the face" every time he and the Tick got into a fight with the forces of evil.

"Can't you put it on something like *Murder She Wrote*?"

"It's *The Tick*, I am so not changing it."

"Is this what I'm going to have to watch for the next six months?"

"It's only on for a half an hour. Don't bitch. Enjoy it. You might actually learn something."

So my mother sat there. She watched *The Tick*. To my surprise, she laughed. We actually found something in common. Who would have thought a blue, idiotic superhero would do it?

Dinner for us was an argument. I wasn't too hungry and neither was my mother. She wanted to hit a sandwich shop at the Navy hospital, I wanted to hit McDonald's. I reminded her that I was the sick one and that I should eat what I wanted to, even if it might kill me in twenty years. She reminded me that she was paying for dinner and that I had better compromise.

"Why not McDonald's today and we hit the town tomorrow night then?" I pleaded.

"Why do you want McDonald's so bad?"

"Because I do. I just need something simple and I'm feeling like shit. McDonald's is down over the hill. The sandwich shop is way the hell over there."

"Ok, you win. But tomorrow we get some crab cakes." My mother had this thing for Maryland crab cakes. She had to have them. Not sure where she picked up this hunger for crab, but if that was what she wanted then I might as well humor her. After all she was down here with me.

Before we hit McDonald's we beamed on over to the Navy Commissary for some supplies. A Journey tape for my walkman and a Justice League trade paperback for my entertainment. My mother grabbed a couple of books. The cashier who rang us up was this beautiful woman from Russia. Her husband must have worked on the base, but she had me enthralled. I almost asked for a phone number. It took an impatient, fat Navy wife bumping my pump and causing it to tug on my central line to bring me back to reality.

"Damn, be careful please."

"Oh, what? Did you say something?" She acted all stupid.

"Yeah I did, I said watch where you are going! Want me to spell it for you, Ma'am?"

She gave me this horrified look and people glared at me. It was an odd moment. They stared at my pump and my neck. My mother was waiting for me by the door. "What? I take it you've never seen a cancer patient before? Well get a good look at me while you can." I was extremely pissed. How rude of people to look at me like some circus freak. I was a human being and I was a sailor. Wait, a sailor with cancer? Kinda dumb. My military programming kicked in and I walked out of the commissary, biting my lip to prevent another outburst.

"You ok?" my mother asked.

"I can't believe that bitch."

"Some people just don't understand."

"Well she should have paid attention. As for everyone else, what the fuck?"

"You have a pump hooked up to you and a big IV in your neck. That causes people to want to stare. Just ignore it."

Misery Likes Company

I sometimes think I survived cancer just to preach to those who suck at life. At other times I think there might have been a higher calling. Either way, I fucked it all up pretty good. When I returned home from my first round of EPOCH II, I was quick to visit Leanna. I needed her smile. I needed her energy. I just needed her. I was miserable. My tongue tasted like chemo. Bland, raw and sick. Leanna could change that. Well, maybe not long term, but short term.

"Hey there!" I slapped my hand on the Orange Julius counter.

"Hey, Jay." All the girls at the juice place knew me. Jess, the assassin, Liz, and Leanna were all there. Leanna, as always came from behind the counter and gave me a hug.

"Did you miss me?" I smiled. I was at peace for a moment.

"Of course." Leanna gave me a kiss on my lips. Bliss? Maybe. It felt like it. I could smell pretzels on her breath, Leanna's favorite snack.

"Do you mean it?"

"Yes."

"Good. I needed that." I gave Leanna another big squeeze. "So what's the plan for tonight?"

"Blockbuster, then my house."

"Ah, a night of couch movies and pizza. Good deal."

I spent the rest of the afternoon walking around the mall, taking in the sights and sounds. It was the after-Christmas chaos, but I still liked it. When Leanna got out of work we hit Blockbuster. The place in South Portland was busy, but it didn't matter. Snow was on the way. A big storm was brewing. The sky was dark, the birds were nowhere to be seen. The streets were empty and the houses had their shades pulled. It was going to be good.

"So what do you want to rent?" Leanna skipped around the store.

"How about Godzilla?" I stood next to the 'For Sale' movies.

"What's that?"

I held up a copy of *Godzilla vs. Megalon*. "This is Godzilla."

"Ok." I could tell Leanna might not be too impressed with my choice. But the video was only five bucks. "But I choose next time."

"No problem, kiddo."

We arrived at Leanna's house around supper time. Brenda was waiting for us at the door. "Jay, your mother called and wants you to call her."

"Sure thing." I went inside and picked up the phone. I had to use my calling card because Leanna didn't have long distance calling. After a barrage of number punching the phone began to ring.

"Hello." My mother answered.

"Hey, did you need something?"

"You need to come home now. There is a storm coming and I don't want you driving in this mess." I looked outside. It was freezing rain in South Portland. "It's not that bad."

"What's wrong?" Leanna whispered.

"My mother is telling me to come home." I responded.

"Mom, can Jay crash on the couch?" Leanna grabbed her mother's arm.

"I don't see why not. Just no hanky panky, you two." Brenda waved her finger at me.

"Sure, no problem. Mom, Brenda said I can crash on the couch here."

"NO! Get your ass home right now!"

"Excuse me? I'll be fine."

"NO! You just had chemo, I want you home! Jason you could get very sick!" My mother yelled even louder.

"Look, Brenda said I can use the couch. I'll be fine."

"Well SHE doesn't know how sick you really are!"

"I'll talk to her." Brenda grabbed the phone from my hands and began chatting with my mother. I was crossing my fingers that my mother didn't tell Brenda how old I was. Brenda went on about being a CNA and how I'd be fine. My mother could be heard tearing up a storm and then Brenda hung up. "Ok, the couch is yours. I'll make up some juice for you. You need to drink lots of liquids tonight."

Leanna gave Brenda a huge hug of happiness and I offered a simple "Thank you." Once the commotion died down the lot of us, with Amy, Leanna's cousin, and Carol, Amy's sister, sat down on the living room floor and popped in Godzilla vs. Megalon.

***

"You are such a Chiki Monkey." The poorly dubbed girl lipped.

"Chiki Monkey?" Leanna looked at me. Amy laughed.

"Yeah, that'd be you. Ah! I can call you that instead of kiddo."

"No way!" Leanna began to pout. Her cheeks looked cute all puffed out.

"Ok Chiki Monkey!" Amy poked Leanna.

"Cut it out Amy or I'll kick your ass!"

"Leanna!" Brenda gave Leanna a funny, but serious look.

"Chiki Monkey!" Carol tried to join in. Amy was about 14, Carol was only about 7 or 8 years old.

"Carol-Anne, they're going to get you. Run to the light!" Leanna snapped back at Carol, whose eyes watered up and ran to her room.

"Leanna, that's enough you Chiki Monkey!" Brenda hit Leanna with a pillow. It was clear that the family of this household did this on a nightly basis.

"Mom, not you too!" Leanna stomped off to her room.

I got up and followed her. Leanna was curled up on her bed. Her room was a closet with a makeshift bed, only separated from the rest of the house by a curtain. On the walls were pictures of her friends, Tweety Bird and other images. "You ok?" I sat next to her and rubbed her back.

"Oh, I'm fine. I can't believe you called me that."

"Well, Chiki Monkey, it does fit you. You are blond, and have sexy curves like a banana and well you're cute. So why not?" I don't think Leanna had ever been complimented without some type of expectation by the person doing the complimenting. As for me, well Leanna was a friend, someone who was sharing in my personal hell.

"Really?"

"Yeah. Come out. The night is still young."

The end of the evening was pretty simple. Amy and Carol went to bed. Brenda escorted Leanna to her room and gave me the "Stay out of her room" speech. But I wasn't going anywhere. The chemo had set in. I was out of it.

When I awoke in the morning I was greeted by a warm breakfast. Unfortunately, I was in no shape to eat. I never was a morning person. I looked out the window and saw almost two feet of snow and some ice on top.

"Want some eggs?" Brenda offered me a plate.

"No, thank you. I need to get home. I'm not feeling so good." Of course I always had morning sickness, but chemo morning sickness sucked ass. I suited up and cleared off my car. Leanna helped, sneaking kisses here and there. Once my car was cleaned off I hopped in and started it up.

"Call me later?"

"Sounds like a plan, Chiki Monkey."

***

I returned to Bethesda a week and a half later with no idea of what was to come. To me, it was just another treatment. But this time I would be confined to a hospital bed, not allowed to leave, not allowed to exist as a normal human. The second round of EPOCH II was the bad one. They said that several patients died from this cycle. I'm not surprised. Before I left, I supplied Leanna with a calling card. She told me that her week would consist of school and a party. She was no doubt going to be doing drugs and drinking. Most likely having herself a good time and getting laid. Meanwhile I'd be in a bed, dying. I was jealous.

I did the blood draw, the CT, and the vitals. From there I was admitted to the In-Patient Oncology unit at NIH. I was placed in a room by myself. I tried to get comfortable, but the room wasn't too friendly. A small TV on a metal beam that was movable was the only entertainment that I had. The nurses were cold. Not as friendly as Karen and the rest of the outpatient staff.

"I'm going to head back to the hotel for the night" my mother told me. "If you need me, call." My mother looked ill. She knew more than I did.

"Sure thing. Watch *The Tick* for me." I waved goodbye and I was alone.

The first thing that should have caused me to panic was when the nurse brought in the chemo drugs in a glass jar. "That's different."

"It's because the chemical is so acidic it can eat through plastic."

"So how is it going to handle my IV?"

"Well, if you feel a burning sensation outside of the normal burning that you feel, then call us."

"That's very reassuring. In other words you're going to be pumping battery acid into my blood." I shook my head.

"I guess you could put it that way. We will be administering this drug over the next 6 hours. Any faster and it could kill you."

"Nice." My heart skipped a few beats. "Anything else I should know?"

"Yes, here, sign this." The nurse handed me a release form that covered what this drug could do to me. Immediate death was a side effect that stuck out the most. I picked up the pen and signed.

"Let's do this." I nodded.

"Ok, I will be in on and off checking your vitals. If you feel anything strange call us. This is going to make you extremely ill. Most patients go neutropenic within days of this cycle."

"Well, I guess you didn't read the doctor's notes from the CHOP. My body loves to fight off chemo drugs, so bring it." I was defiant and there was nothing that was going to bring me down.

I watched as the nurse opened the line and the poison slipped down the plastic tube and into my body. I felt ill right that instant. By body warmed up and my temp spiked two degrees. My nose felt like it was bleeding, an electric taste shot through my nostrils. My skin started to turn red. The nurse checked my pulse, smiled and left the room. On the way out she dimmed the lights.

Needing a distraction, I pulled the TV over and switched it on. NIH had crappy cable. No Tick, no nothing, just black television sitcoms and a select group of censored movies. I clicked over to the TV guide station that NIH had. *Star Trek First Contact* was about to begin. While it was a sore spot in my life since that was the film Dawn and I saw on our first date, it was violent and exciting. I needed that. What I didn't realize is how badly that film would fuck me up each time I watched it after this whole ordeal. L. Ron Hubbard talks about this in his book **Dianetics**, about recall causing people to literally freeze in terror and have flashbacks. The opening theme of *First Contact* played as my body experienced several violent reactions. I started to cry as the burning got worse. I thought I would probably not make it through the night. Then I was ripped away by more misery as I discovered that *First Contact* was censored. Pichard didn't have the Borg thingy busting out of his cheek. Shit, I wasn't going to enjoy the film. I fell asleep feeling very uncomfortable.

About two hours later I was awoken by a phone call. Leanna. "What's up Jay?"

"Not much. Just feeling like shit."

"Hey, Jay!" A familiar voice shouted out in the background. That was followed by a loud cheer of "Hey, Jay!" by a large group of people.

"How's the party?"

"Good, we are having fun. A little drinking, but I'm crashing at Liz's house."

"Ok, just stay out of trouble." Great, here I was sick as a dog and she was partying at home. But it was her life, I was only a small piece of it.

"I will. I love you!" Leanna shouted.

"I love you too, Chiki Monkey." Just then my stomach cramped in a way that I had never experienced before. "Argh, I've got to go." I hung up quickly and hit the nurse call button and waited.

I waited for about ten minutes before a nurse came in. By that time I was on my side crying. The best way to describe the pain would be if someone punched a hole in my stomach and slowly twisted and pulled my intestines out, inch by inch, all while pinching them with pliers.

"Are you ok, Mr. Libby?" The nurse looked annoyed.

"No, this really hurts." It hurt badly enough that I heaved and everything I had eaten that day came up all at once. I choked on my vomit as the nurse ran out of the room. I couldn't breath and my head was spinning like I had just done a 360 degree turn at mach 10. I started to heave again and a friendly voice whispered in my ear, another nurse placed a basin under my face as I let loose bile.

"Jason, use this, honey." I looked up, my face drenched with tears, and there stood a Middle Eastern nurse with a gentle smile and comforting brown eyes.

"Oh God, it hurts. I didn't expect this."

"This is normal. If you want we can give you morphine."

"No, morphine makes me sick."

"Would you like something else?"

"No, God did this to me for a reason, I will tough it out."

"Honey, I don't think God did this to you. And if He did, I'm sure He doesn't want you to suffer like this."

"You have no idea how much I deserve this. I'll suffer and it'll make me stronger."

The nurse stepped away from me. My eyes were glazing over. The room was blurred and it felt like the flames of hell were scorching my skin. "We might need to stop," the nurse said.

"NO! The bottle is almost done. Let's finish this." I sat up and held my stomach as wave after wave of pain shot through me. "It's a good day to die."

The next morning I was exhausted. After being up all night in tears, enduring the pain and vomiting nothing but my stomach, I was ready to sleep. No such luck. About 7am the nursing staff came in for vitals. "Feeling any better?"

"You tell me. Have you ever been through this?"

"No, but..."

"Yeah, exactly. I'm alive. That's all that needs to be said."

I was offered a breakfast menu and I checked off some bread-eat products and juice. In reality, I never ate breakfast other than when the Navy required me to. The tray was brought to my room but I didn't eat. I was too sick.

My discharge was pretty simple. My step-father had been in contact with Mercy hospital and Doctor K, a man who was respected and well-known in Portland for his temper and his excellent patient care. Doctor K agreed to monitor me while I was in Maine. In addition, an oncologist from Central Maine Medical Center was also onboard. He had done a residency at NIH with Doctor Wilson. All I needed to do was get my blood drawn and stick myself with a needle every morning until my counts went back up. I sat in the outpatient clinic as the nurse requested I demonstrate how to stick myself in the stomach. Neupogen was the newest great thing to bring up your white counts.

"Warm it to room temperature about five minutes before sticking yourself. Be careful, these bottles are worth about $450 a pop." The nurse held up a tiny vial. "Each night or morning you need to inject this into your leg or stomach, wherever you have body fat." She handed me a vial and a small syringe. "Do it."

"No problem." When I had my mind set on being a hospitalman in the Navy, I wasn't kidding around. I knew exactly what to do. I popped the safety cap off and inserted the needle into the soft cap of the vial. Once I filled the syringe, I evacuated the tiny bit of air inside by flicking the side of the syringe until all the air bubbles surfaced. I then applied pressure to the plunger to leak the bubbles out until a little drop of Neupogen appeared. I put the syringe in my mouth and tore open the alcohol prep pad, pulled my shirt up and wiped a spot on my stomach. I then grabbed the syringe. "Let's rock and roll!" I stabbed myself in the stomach and injected the drug.

"Done like a real pro." The nurse smiled.

"You know it." I winked and stood up. My body was very weak from the chemo and I almost fell over.

"You'll need a wheelchair for about a day. And don't be surprised if your hip bones throb from the Neupogen. It's common."

"Oh, great, I have to wheel you to the jetport." My mother, who had been silent during the whole debriefing, shook her head. We were given a small cooler with about eight vials of Neupogen, a bag of syringes and alcohol prep pads. "Airport security is going to love us."

"At least we don't have a bomb."

***

Within two days of getting home I went neutropenic. I was taken to Mercy Hospital and admitted through the ER. It was like a bad dream. The room I was placed in was by the nurse's station. It was an isolation room to designed to keep germs out. The room itself was bland, with a window that offered a view of a brick wall. Luckily there was a large television set. An IV was inserted into my arm and I was left to dwell.

I was totally alone, but that was short lived. Leanna's mom dropped her off for the day to keep me company.

"How are you feeling?"

"Well, Chiki Monkey, I guess not too bad. I just think it sucks that I got laid up so fast."

"Looks like you won't make it to my dance." Leanna looked disappointed, but it was not like I would have been able to go anyway.

"Well, go have a good time. I'm not going anywhere and I don't want you to feel like you have to be with me 24/7."

"I'll tell you what, I'll come in after the dance to see you."

"That sounds great, Chiki Monkey." She gave me a hug and sat down next to my bed.

Programming was limited to VH1 and TNT, although we scored big with a Discovery Channel program about exorcisms. Hell, I was already heading to the land down under. Leanna held my hand. Part-way through the programming a nurse came into the room. She wasn't dressed the way a traditional nurse should be dressed, with scrubs and rubber shoes. She was dressed in dark colors, but she looked like she had some type of command. Her hair was semi-curled and it hung about neck length. She was beautiful. I winked at Leanna.

"Mr. Libby, my name is Sister Mary." My heart just about stopped, it was a Sister of Mercy. I had heard tales about the nuns from my stepfather who at one point was the head nurse at Mercy. They were wild and crazy. Sister Mary stood next to the bed. "And who is this lovely young lady with you?"

"This is Leanna, or more famously known as Chiki Monkey." Leanna stood up and shook Sister Mary's hand.

"Nice to meet you, Sister Mary." Leanna was picking up on good manners quickly.

"So what are you two kids watching?" Sister Mary looked at the TV as it showed pictures of ancient carvings depicting devils.

"It's a show on the history of exorcisms. You can watch it with us if you'd like." The idea was to scare away the nun. I was far from religious. Sister Mary checked my IV line, listened to my lungs and looked down my throat.

Sister Mary seemed like she was leaving, but instead she pulled up the chair that was sitting next to the door. "I love shows like this."

So there the three of us sat watching a show about pea soup spitting teens, African tribes and Jesus. Leanna poked my arm and pointed to Sister Mary whose eyes were locked onto the TV screen like she was entranced. Her smile was beautiful and she kept looking our way. "This is great. Do you have a religion, Jason?"

"I used to be a Bible thumping Protestant until our church Pastor called me a Pagan because I did Indian dances for Boy Scouts."

"That's too bad. Would you like to speak to a Priest?"

"Not really Sister. I don't need God gloating over my punishment."

"What do you mean?"

"God is punishing me for all the bad things I have done in my life. I don't want to repent or try to be saved. Other people deserve it more than I do."

"That's not true, everyone can be saved."

"Not me, I have broken eight of the Ten Commandments, I'm finished. But thanks for the offer."

Sister Mary patted my hand and held it while we continued to watch the show. Leanna stood up and picked up her purse. "I'm going to go get a soda, do you want anything?"

"No thanks Chiki Monkey."

"No thank you sweety." Sister Mary smiled. Leanna walked out of the room. "She is a very sweet girl."

"She is just a teenager, Sister."

"So, she is here for you. Does she know how bad it is?"

"I've tried to tell her. I'm not sure if she fully understands yet. I want her to enjoy her teen years, not sit here with me while I die."

"That is tough, but maybe she'll understand. She's old enough to make her own decisions."

"I know. I guess it's just because I've always pushed people away when I was sick."

"Well don't be too hard on yourself. A lot of people are praying for you."

"Save your prayers for someone who needs them. If I beat this it will be because I willed it."

Sister Mary leaned over and gave me a kiss on the cheek. "God bless you. I'll still pray." She turned her head back to the TV. "Do you really think this is true?"

"I've seen some messed up things, but I think half of the demonic possessions are just people crying out for attention. But there are things out there. I've seen them."

Sister Mary looked back at me. I told her the tale of the ghost in the well. How I heard a little girl calling for help from inside. How I pulled the rotten wood from the top while another firefighter grabbed my feet. How I lowered my top half into the well, reaching for this little girl. A flashlight was handed to me and when I turned it on the well was empty. We talked about that night for years. Sister Mary looked chilled when I finished.

"Freaky, huh?"

"That is amazing. You have really touched the other side."

"Maybe, but I would prefer not going there."

Leanna came back in and Sister Mary stood up. "I suppose I ought to get some work done. I'll check up on you later."

"Thank you Sister."

"Did you two have fun while I was gone?"

"Oh you know it." I laughed and Leanna sat down in her seat.

"Well, I need to get going. I need to get ready for the dance."

"Ok Chiki Monkey. I'll catchya later then."

Leanna leaned over and gave me a huge hug. "I love you."

"Love you too, now get out of here. I'll see you tomorrow."

Leanna left and I was alone. I didn't feel angry this time. Sister Mary had really healed some wounds just by sitting with me. So the rest of my evening I sat around and watched VH1. Dave Matthews and Hanson became my musical entertainment, while the Spice Girls made me horny and depressed. No sex for me. I fell asleep.

***

They say that angels come to see you when you are dying. I say that they are full of it. But that night while I slept a soft voice pulled me out of my deep sleep. "Jay, wake up." I felt a softness on my forehead, a feeling of moistness and love. My eyes opened slowly. Standing in the shadows was a beautiful form, shrouded in a purple gown. She almost glowed. I was very drowsy and could hardly keep myself awake.

"Are you an angel?" I asked as I reached out.

"Better than that." She stepped into the light created by the IV pump and placed my hand over her heart. Tears formed in her eyes and the twinkle of glitter on her skin sparkled different colors. She leaned over and touched her lips to mine. We kissed for about a minute and then she stepped back. "So what do you think?"

"Leanna? It's you. I thought you were an angel. You look so beautiful."

"Really?"

"You are the best thing I have woken to ever. You must have been radiant at the dance. But how did you get in here?"

"I just did." She came closer and kissed me again. I put my arms around Leanna and just held her. It was all I could do.

"Love you."

I drifted back to sleep with a smile on my face. She had come to see me, my own personal angel. I couldn't believe it. I figured she would have forgotten about me, but Leanna was much more dedicated than I realized. My dreams that night were ones of a future together.

I stayed in the hospital for about three days. Doctor K came to see me on and off. He would walk in and ask how I was doing. Then he'd walk out, but at least I'd know what was going on. Doctor K was good about honesty. When my time was up at Mercy I went home for two weeks of R&R and spent most of that time with Leanna catching movies at the Nickelodeon. Before I knew it I had to go back to Bethesda for more chemo.

***

My mother was becoming a pain in the ass at NIH. My third round of chemo was just like the first. I got a central line and then walked around with an IV bag.

"You look so cute with your purse."

"Oh, thanks." I shook my head, but a pain in my neck brought me back to the reality that a long IV was in my neck.

"That's good, go ahead and turn your neck like that." She mocked me as I held my neck.

"Keep this shit up and I'll have you watching *South Park*." I swiped the remote to the TV as we entered our hotel room at the Navy Lodge.

"What's *South Park*?" she inquired.

"It's a very fucked up cartoon."

"Oh, like *The Tick*?"

"Not quite, just watch tonight."

The rest of our short day consisted of McDonald's and an evening of Comedy Central and my mother's introduction to Mr. Hanky.

"Oh my GOD Jason!" My mother laughed in disgust.

"Yeah, Mr. Hanky, the Christmas Poo." I laughed hard until my neck started to ache.

"Who the hell came up with this?"

"Don't worry about it." She reached for the remote, but I quickly grabbed it, "just enjoy the rest of the show."

After *South Park* was over we watched the DC news. One thing Washington, DC is never short of is crime. Reports of shootings, car jackings, murders and racial tensions consumed the full four hours of just LOCAL news.

"That was just down the street from here." My mother sounded worried.

"And just think it was an armed bank robbery. The murder happened about five miles from that." Life/death had no meaning to me. A good soldier forgets the value of life in order to function during war. The Navy didn't do much for me in the area of brainwashing. I shut away my feelings the minute I stepped on the bus for Great Lakes. I was ready to die, and if someone tried to rob me they had better ask themselves the same question. I loved it in Bethesda.

"How can you joke about that?"

"Because I can. I'm in the fucking military, not the Boy Scouts."

"Obviously. I see your twisted sense of humor."

"What?" I stood up and began the long task of taking my shirt off with an IV pump attached to me.

"Need some help?"

"I'm not crippled." I snaked the pump bag through my collar and back onto the bed. "See, easy as Π."

"I didn't say you were. God you can be such a pain sometimes."

"Why, thank you. I do try." I winked and moved myself into the bathroom in order to wash up.

How do you wash yourself with a central line? Well the easiest way is to take a sponge bath. Or you can tape it up. I was always fond of the combo. My hair was important to me, even though it was already coming out. I turned on the tub and set the water to a comfortable warm. Then I placed the IV pump on the toilet seat next to me and kneeled. Like a Frenchman getting ready to hit the guillotine, I lowered my head under the water and rinsed my hair. Then like a pro, I reached one-handed for the hotel soap and unwrapped it. It smelled like flowers, but it would do. I rubbed it on my scalp and created minimal suds. For some reason, the water in Bethesda didn't like soap. Once I finished covering my hair in a nice layer, I began the one-handed rinsing process. Remember that I was also holding myself up with one arm. My knees were throbbing. Once the soap was gone I stood up and my limbs creaked.

"I'm getting too old for this." I looked at myself in the mirror. My scars were bright red, even the zipper on my chest. The EPOCH II was starting to really do a number on me. "Man, I look like shit."

"Did you say something?" My mother heard me.

"I said I look like shit."

"Well you are going through chemo, what do you expect to look like?"

"Good point." I noticed most of my chest hair was almost gone again. "At least I get to go through puberty again."

"Ok, well I need to hit the sack."

"Do you think this will help me get laid?" I was always blunt around my mother.

"Maybe if it's a high school girl." She gave me a look. I knew she was talking about Leanna. Speaking of Leanna! I grabbed my calling card and dialed the magic numbers.

"Hello." Amy, Leanna's cousin answered.

"Hey this is Jay is Leanna in?"

"Yeah, but I'm on the other line."

"Amy, I'm calling from DC."

"Can she call you back?"

"Sure, whatever. Here is my number." I gave her the number and hung up.

"No luck?"

"Fucking Amy, talking to her boyfriend." I was slightly pissed. Amy was always on the phone.

"Well, get some sleep."

"Sure." I sat there for about an hour until the phone rang. My mother was alseep.

"Hello." I whispered.

"Hi, Jay. Amy just gave me the message you called."

"I called over an hour ago."

"You WHAT!?" I heard Leanna get up from her bed and storm into another room, it was that loud. "AMY! You told me he just called!"

"He did," Amy tried to respond. I heard scuffling and then Brenda yelling at them both.

"Mom, Amy's been on the phone all night. And she didn't bother to tell me Jay called."

Teenage issues. My god. I didn't hold it against Amy that she wanted to talk to her man, but not giving the message to Leanna for over an hour was rude. "Easy there Leanna."

"Leanna, hang up the phone now and go to your room!"

"But Jay is on the line!"

"Say goodnight, Leanna!" Brenda sounded pissed.

"Fine! I have go."

"It's ok, Chiki Monkey." I tried to calm her down. "Call me tomorrow at the number I gave Amy."

"Ok." Leanna sounded really upset. "I missed you a lot today. I wrote you a note too."

"Get some sleep. I love you."

"Ok, I love you too." Leanna hung up and I put my head down on the hotel pillow. The starchy texture drove me nuts. I needed my feather pillows and cold air. The room temperature was way too warm. I tossed and turned all night.

***

I sometimes think that the simplest creatures have it easy in comparison to the human race. My view comes from the ducklings at the Navy Lodge. They waddled around looking for bread crumbs and other scraps. Scrounging, yes. Suffering no.

"Do you want to feed them?" My mother asked as she puffed away on a cigarette. She had in her hand bread left over from a Subway sandwich. She was pinching off pieces and rolling them into a ball with her fingers. The ducklings and the mother duck waddled right up to her and squawked with an eagerness to be fed.

"Looks like you are doing just fine." I wasn't up for feeding the ducks. While they were a distraction I had two things on my mind: Leanna, and the next hospital stay.

"Suit yourself."

"Besides, I wouldn't want to get some killer germ from them." I smiled my usual smile and planted myself on the sidewalk next to the small duck pond. When I say small, I mean really small. It had to have been about five feet wide and six feet long. It was more like an engineer's mistake that the Navy was too cheap to fix. The ducks must have found it by chance.

"Don't be foolish." My mother scolded me. I had grown up on Sebago Lake. I was always around the ducks.

"Alright, toss me some bread." I reached out. My mother threw me a couple chunks. The ducklings chased after the bread. I picked it up and started to break off small pieces and dropped them about two feet from me. A couple drove up and looked at me in disgust. City people couldn't appreciate such natural beauty like a duckling. That soft yellow fuzz, the little black legs and those tiny beaks. There was no ugly duckling here, only my mother, the mother duck, myself and the ducklings. Ironic. Mother and son, and mother and children, all together bonding even if we were from a different species. I put a piece of bread in my hand and tried to get a duckling to take it from me. But it didn't happen. The city folks must have terrified them one too many times. The ducklings were friendly, but not trusting. I ended up dropping the piece on the grass.

"They are cute aren't they?" My mother took one last drag and dropped her cigarette on the pavement and put it out with the tip of her shoe.

"Yep. I wish I was a duckling." I stood up and brushed myself off. "That way I could just waddle around all day and not have an IV bag strapped to me." I put my arms at my side like wings and waddled a little. The central line in my neck pulled. The reminder, I was not a duckling. I was Jay, and I was sick.

"Oh my God, I don't know you." My mother looked embarrassed. She should have been. Here I was, an adult acting like a duckling, waddling around with other ducklings. Her response prompted me to let out a quacking sound. The mother duck waddled over to me and responded.

"Quack, quack." I lowered myself down trying not to act intimidating. The mother duck waddled up to me and let out another quack, and I responded with the same. We did this for a few minutes. Neither of us knew what each other was saying, but my mother finally turned away and headed back to the main entrance up on the hill.

"I'll see you inside, Jason."

"Wait up." I straightened my back and the mother duck jumped. "This conversation is going nowhere anyway."

"You worry me."

"I should." I laughed. "I can talk with the animals."

"I don't know you." My mother said again and went inside.

I followed behind her and then turned to my friends, the ducks. They looked at me, with those begging eyes. I don't know if they wanted more food or more conversation. I met the mother duck's eyes with my own, offering a look of forgiveness and sorrow. "Sorry, all out." I shrugged. The mother duck quacked and the ducklings grouped together and marched back to the pond.

***

That night I called Leanna on her Track phone. When she answered I heard tons of noise, she was at a party.

"Hey, Gummy!" Her nickname she had given me. God knows why, I was almost 170lbs. But maybe it was from my consumption of Gummy Bears.

"What's up, Chiki Monkey?" My heart sank. Leanna and parties were not a good thing.

"Jess and I are camping with some of her friends and doing a little drinking." She didn't sound drunk, thank God.

"Stay out of trouble, please and don't drink too much." I just wanted to be with her instead of in the hotel room.

"I will!" I heard some male voices and then Jess.

"We miss you, Jay!" Jess screamed in the background.

"Tell Jess I miss her too." I really began to wonder.

"Jay says he misses you too!" Leanna laughed.

"We miss you too, Jay!" two male voices yelled out in the background. I heard Leanna 'Shh' them.

"I love you, Chiki Monkey. I'll see you when I get home." With that I hung up. I didn't even want to think about what might be going on. I sat on my bed and stared at the TV.

"Are you ok?" My mother noticed I was pissed.

"Yeah, Leanna and Jess are having a little camping party with some guys and they are drinking."

"That's not right, but what do you expect?" My mother didn't like Leanna. I'm not sure if it was Leanna's age or the fact that I had high regard for Leanna well above what I ever had for her.

"I don't know. I don't like the fact that she is drinking for one. But even if I look past it, I don't like the fact that there are guys there." I tried to get comfortable. My neck was throbbing from the central line and the room was too warm.

"You need to focus on getting better, not that little girl."

"She's not a little girl. Jesus, can't you come up with something a little more supportive?" I grabbed a pillow and put it over my head and closed my eyes.

***

The doctors informed me that I would probably be Neutropenic within the first week of being home because my body was breaking down. So, if I was going to do anything, I had to plan. I decided that I'd set Jess and Jason up on a date. Leanna was all for it. I wanted one of my friends around Leanna when I was gone, someone I could trust, someone that could keep an eye on her. Setting Jason up with Jess would be perfect.

As soon as I returned to Maine, I picked Leanna up at her house.

"Gummi!" She smiled at me, such an innocent look to her, but Leanna was far from that. Brenda stood behind her.

"Welcome home, Jay." She waved.

"Thank you, Ms. Jordan." I waved with one hand as Leanna clung onto me and kissed my cheek.

"How are you feeling?" Brenda walked down the stairs in the

front of Leanna's house and gave me a hug.

"Everything tastes like cream soda still." I made a gross face. It was true. All the chemo had done a number on my taste buds. Everything tasted like cream soda, something I hated with a passion.

"Do you want some mints?" While I didn't care for some of her parenting habits, Brenda was caring and like a second mother. She would have made a fun mother in-law.

"No thank you. We're going to hit Chili's and get some spicy Mexican food." I winked and back stepped to the Jeep. Leanna followed, almost skipping. I opened the door for her and let her get situated in the passenger seat.

"It's a school night, Leanna. Don't be out late." Brenda waved her finger.

"Mom, give me a break." Leanna whined.

"I'll have her back by nine." I started up the Jeep and gave Brenda a thumbs up.

There was one thing that I needed from Leanna, and that was for her to get plenty of sleep and keep up on her school work. I couldn't interfere with her life on a level that would ruin it. Not that cancer was any better of a distraction.

"So, we need to connect Jay and Jess somehow." I rubbed Leanna's knee. She was wearing a pair of red sport shorts. The temptation to go further up was there, but I needed to maintain control.

"How about a camping trip?" Leanna suggested.

"Yeah, but where? It can't be too far away." I pulled out my Maine map from the glove box as we drove down the road. "We could always hit the property out behind my parent's house. Thirty acres is a lot of land."

"That sounds like fun." Leanna hugged my arm. "I'll call Jess when we get to my house."

"Cool, I'll buzz Jay later." I leaned over and kissed Leanna.

"Who's buying the drinks?" Leanna gave me a look.

"No one." I shook my head. "How about a dry run and just have fun around a camp fire?"

Leanna looked disappointed. Oh well. She wasn't even eighteen and I wasn't going to buy beer for her. I wanted to be with friends, not drinking buddies. Jason was the same way. We'd do sterno and marshmallows, along with a couple cans of Coke.

"Are you sure?" Leanna pried.

"No offense, Chiki Monkey, but I only have a few days of out time. If I drink I could land at Mercy a lot quicker."

"Ok. You have a good point. I want to have you out as long as I can." Leanna gave me a quick kiss and sat back.

***

Setting my friend Jason up on a blind date wasn't easy. Jess was a cutie, but she had a wild streak. Jason, on the other hand, had been my party buddy and best friend since we were Boy Scouts. We had never been separated for long. My senior year he was in boot camp for the Army. When I went to Great Lakes for the Navy, he ended up at Drexel University. Soon afterwards, I was in Philadelphia with him. We drank, partied, did the uber bar thing and had a blast. When I came back to Maine with cancer, Jason soon followed. He was my guardian angel of sorts. A born again uber Christian whose church was more like a cult. But Jason still listened to Manowar, so he wasn't lost.

Jason sat on my computer chair while I sat on my mattress on the floor in my bedroom. Well, it was like a bedroom. It was a mattress, a TV, computer and boxes with books. My parent's attempt to have me die in a room that they didn't use that often. The ceiling was slanted to an angle which I always hit my head on. Not a great room for someone tall. Jason picked up one of my Star Wars Role-playing Game books (from West End Games) and flipped through some pages.

"Hey, want to go on a blind date?" I smiled. Jason gave me a look.

"It's a camping trip, Jay." My smile turned to an evil grin.

"You're smiling. That isn't a good thing." Jason responded with apprehension.

"Jess is cute." My Jedi mind trick was wavering.

"Did you sleep with her?" Jason knew me well.

"Umm, nope. Never had the chance. I think she's still a virgin." I slapped Jason's shoulder.

"I don't care about that. I just don't want one of your psycho women." Jason laughed.

"Jay, have I ever led you astray?" My horns began to show.

"Jay, when haven't you?" His halo began to shine.

"Look, Jay."

"No, you look, Jay."

"No you, Jay."

"Just a campout. A little sterno, mellows and Coke." I put my hands together like I was praying.

"Ok, but if she turns out to be a nutcase you're going to get it."

Jason made a fist and laughed.

"Deal." I pulled the book from Jason's hands.

"Hey, I was looking at that." Jason grabbed it back from me.

"No way!" I smacked his hand. "I don't want you reading the rules."

"What, so I'd actually see that you don't know them?" Jason and I laughed.

"Well, yeah."

***

That evening we all met at the post office at the junction of Route 11 and Route 25 in Limington. Jason in his car, Leanna and myself in the Jeep and Jess with her lemon-mobile. Jess looked a little dolled up. She was always beautiful, even if she was the product of the Bereans, a group of Christians who I felt had too much time on their hands. Jason was decked out in his camping outfit, jeans, sweatshirt and cap. The air was cold for June. I was bundled up pretty good. Jason and Jess shook hands and we loaded up. Three cars into the forest of Limington. Well, not really. Up one road and off onto a logging road I had scoped out earlier in the day. A fire pit dug and left behind from teen partygoers offered a landmark to camp around. The roads were muddy from the rain.

"Jay, this is soaked. All the wood is." Jess tossed a wet branch into the fire pit.

"You ain't seen nothing yet." I opened the back of the Jeep and dug around. There in a paper bag were two chrome cylinders. There were no markings on them, just a simple lid, like a paint can.

"Oh, here we go!" Jason clapped his hands. "The sterno!"

"What's sterno?" Leanna asked. The two girls cuddled up on a blanket that they had brought.

"God's gift to wayward campers." Jason threw a bunch of wood together and constructed one badass structure.

I cracked open one of the cans with a big knife. Inside a yellowish gel awaited the touch of flame. I picked up a stick off the ground scooped out a giant glob of sterno. I wiped it on the lower parts of the wooden structure that Jason had built. I did it with such pleasure. Man created fire, with some help from nature. I was going to create fire with some help from sterno.

"Think you have enough?" Jason planted himself down on a log.

"One can never have enough sterno!" I raised the stick like an Indian, looking for a sign from the clouds. I ran back to the Jeep and grabbed a lighter, using the bag that had housed the sterno and lit it up. I took my sterno stick and jabbed it into the bag creating a light glaze of flame. It was uncanny. The flames were reaching higher and higher into the night sky. Like a professional, I tossed the burning stick into the wooden structure. In seconds, it was ablaze. "Let there be FIRE!"

The art of camping is always better with a sterno fire. Blue flames flickering around piles of soon to be dead wood. What better way to thank the Gods than to do an Indian dance around the fire to celebrate! Toe, heel, toe heel, arms up and arms down. My audience laughed.

"Ok, Jay. Sit down." Jason slapped his hand on the log on which he was sitting.

"Have a Moxie, Jay." Jess tossed me a can, which I caught but held far away from me.

"Just like the old days." Jason had this look. He seemed to drift away for a moment, then he came back.

"At least it isn't raining." I looked up at the sky.

"Not yet." Jason shook his head.

The rest of our evening went great. After Jason left, Leanna, Jess and I got into the back of the Jeep and snuggled up. One guy, two girls, it would have been ideal. I stress, would have, I was sick. The Gods let loose a downpour upon the white Jeep, nestled in the woods of Limington. Leanna went into the rain to go pee, I followed. We sang in the rain that night.

Shortly afterward we came back to the Jeep. Jess was sitting in her car. "Did you two have fun?"

"I'm probably going to have pneumonia." I shivered. I was getting that feeling, when your body is so cold through and through that you know a cold is soon to come.

"I'll warm you up." Leanna gave me a huge hug. Water poured out of my shirt.

"I'm going to leave you two and go for a drive. I'll be back in a bit." Jess didn't look ok. She actually seemed distraught.

"Be careful, Jess." I bent my head back and let the rain smack my cheeks. "It's coming down pretty hard."

"I will." Jess started up her car and began to back up.

Leanna waved to her. Jess leaving worried me.

"Is she going to be ok?" I asked Leanna.

"I'll call her in a little bit. She has some stuff going on." Leanna did seem concerned.

After snuggling up for a couple hours, Leanna sat up. "Jess isn't back yet, Jay."

I was partly asleep, but opened my eyes enough to see a vacant spot next to the Jeep. "Give her a call."

Leanna took out her phone and dialed. No signal. The price of camping out in Limington. Leanna tried again and hit END. "I can't get a signal."

"Ok, buckle up. We'll drive down to the main road." I climbed over the driver's seat and sat down. The steering wheel was cold and I was shivering. Getting out from under the blanket was a bad idea.

We reached Route 11 and Leanna tried again. Now she had a signal, but no answer. "Nothing. Jay, I'm worried. It's not like Jess."

"Well let's head towards her house and see if she is there." It was a long drive to Jess's house. Twenty minutes later and still no Jess anywhere. I looked at the clock. 4 a.m. and we hadn't spotted anyone.

After dialing Jess's cell about thirty times, Leanna started dialing another number. "I'm calling her house."

I could hear the phone ringing then a voice. Leanna asked for Jess and her face went ghost white. "Oh my God!"

"What?"

"Jess was in an accident. She's at Maine Med." Leanna started to cry.

"Are you serious?" I couldn't believe what I was hearing.

"Can you take me to the hospital?" Leanna asked.

"Yeah, no problem." I rubbed Leanna's shoulder. I felt responsible for what was happening and I should have. With the weather this bad I should have told Jess to stay.

***

"Man, my throat is killing me." I rubbed my neck.

Chief Johnson looked at me. "Is it because you stayed up all night?"

"No, but I suppose it didn't help." I tried to cough up some flem.

"How's your friend doing?" Chief shuffled some papers on his desk.

"She's ok, but she won't be doing supermodel work for a bit." He was referring to Jess, who left the campout early in the morning only to get into a very bad accident. Leanna and I had spent all night looking for her. I hadn't gotten much sleep and being wet from the rain was a very bad thing.

"That's too bad. But at least she's alive, Lib." Chief picked up the phone. "Doc, come in and take a look at Lib's throat."

"Really, I'll be ok." I tried to cough again, but everything was tight.

Doc Weidman came in. He was about thirty-five years old. His expertise was as a corpsman, which made him very useful. He felt my neck, looked down my throat and then gave Chief a not so confident look, shaking his head. "He's really sick."

"Tell me something I don't know." Chief chuckled.

"No kidding, Doc. I do have cancer." We all laughed. Chief liked to keep morale at the command high. A fun-loving, military atmosphere was good for everyone. I considered it McHale's Navy.

"I'd suggest taking it easy before your counts drop." Doc looked at Chief.

"Lib, get out."

I stood up, saluted and walked out of the office. I paused. I wanted to hear what was being said.

"Seriously, Chief. He needs to be in the hospital. I've been on the horn with his doctors in Bethesda. Lib's got it bad." Doc paused.

"What am I supposed to do? The kid wants to work."

"Give him the rest of the week off then. If his counts bottom out when he is sick like this it could kill him."

"LIBBY, GO HOME!" Chief Johnson shouted.

"Aye, aye." I responded. I could use the sleep. But rest was limited. I was leaving for Rangeley for the Fourth of July.

***

I think my Step-Mother Joan's parents invited me to Rangeley for the 'all you can eat lobster cookout' because I was really sick. One of those deals where you want to get to know someone before they go. My dad gave me the invite. As a lobster fiend, I knew that it was my calling. My throat was almost swollen shut. I could hardly swallow. But I would manage. I even brought Leanna up with me. But there was something lurking in her closet.

"Why is it you've been acting weird lately" I asked Leanna, as we drove to the camp on Rangeley Lake. The mountains were intimidating indeed. You could look to one side of the road and see an almost dead drop down the side of the mountain. I got dizzy just looking at it.

"I haven't been." Leanna leaned over and tried looking at the view. The Rangely Lakes were a sight to behold from the top of the mountain. Green forest, blue skies and a dark blue lake with islands peppered across it.

"Why is it you have been so reluctant to let me touch you?" I pried.

"No, I haven't."

"Did something happen at the party?" I dug further. Leanna's face got the look. Yes, THE look. Like she had been caught doing something she shouldn't have. "Oh man, what happened?"

"Don't worry about it." Leanna sat back in her seat. She started to look like she was going to cry.

"I will worry. What happened?" I reached over to touch Leanna's hand. She pulled away.

"Drop it, Jay."

"Tell me."

"NO!" Leanna shouted.

"WHAT THE FUCK HAPPENED!" I roared. Leanna jumped in her seat and began to cry. I must have scared the crap out of her. Hell, I scared the crap out of myself.

"I passed out after drinking and woke up with my pants down to my knees." She cried.

"You were raped?" I kept my tone low.

"Yes." Leanna totally lost it. I put my arm around her and pulled her to my shoulder.

"Who did it?"

"I don't know."

"I want a list of every male there. Someone is going to learn a valuable lesson in pain." My anger built up. Someone had raped my girlfriend. They had done something horrific to my lifeline to the real world. Whoever it was would pay. Even if it meant torturing every fucking male who was at the party. I was going to die anyway, I wasn't worried about killing a rapist.

"No, Jay. I'm fine. I'm sorry I didn't tell you." Leanna cried.

"No secrets, that's why we make such a great team." I kissed her forehead. "I need to ask. Do you know if they used a condom?"

"I don't know." She went white.

My heart sank. Any germ, any disease, anything could kill me. Leanna knew it. Yet she didn't tell me. I know why she didn't, she was ashamed enough. "Fuck. FUCK!" I hit the steering wheel. "You know that one wrong germ could kill me, Leanna! Why didn't you FUCKING TELL ME!" I raised my voice again.

"Stop yelling at ME!" Leanna snapped back.

"I'm sorry. It's not your fault. I'm such an ass for yelling." I took a deep breath and exhaled.

***

It was an uneasy Fourth of July. Leanna seemed so distant. I tried to get her to relax, but she was upset. She bonded well with my half-sisters. Cerissa and Ciara were pretty distant from me. Cerissa and I did not get along. I'm not sure why. Ciara and I were a little closer. I spent a lot of time with her that weekend. I wanted to at least have one sister that would know me before I died. It would be her. As for lobster, well let's just say I had my way with over 12 lobster bodies.

"Give the bodies to Jason. He'll eat them." Joan's mother slid over a plate with a nicely cooked lobster body awaiting my fingers.

"Gummi, how's your throat?" Leanna had cuddled up with me at the table.

"Thank God lobster is soft and wet, otherwise this wouldn't be happening." I kissed her cheek and cracked open another body. White lobster meat peaked through at the joints. I picked away.

"I love you." Leanna looked at me. Her eyes were happy. Really happy.

I smiled and kissed her cheek again. "I love you too, Chiki Monkey."

While Ciara, Leanna and I bonded well, I don't think my dad knew what to do. We had always been distant. I can blame my mother for that. Her constant preaching about how horrible my dad was didn't help my view of him. The thing is he wasn't a bad man at all. I had let my mother's hatred get to me, influence me. My dad wasn't a drunk and wasn't in and out of jail. He was a good man. Seeing me ill, after not being part of my life for years must have been an eye opener for him. I held nothing against him. I blamed my mother for the alienation of my father.

***

Alone I'm thinking
Why is Superman Dead
Is it in my head?
~Our Lady Peace

"I need to go pee." Leanna squirmed in her seat.

My dad looked back and laughed. "There's no bathrooms out here, Leanna."

"Jay." Leanna whispered. "I'm going to pee myself."

I tried to whisper to her, but my throat was so swollen that I couldn't. "You heard my dad. No bathrooms out here."

"That's unless you want to use the woods." My dad interjected.

"That's good enough. My bladder is going to pop!" Leanna whimpered.

My dad pulled over into an area that looked like it had been used for ATVs. Leanna jumped out and ran over a dirt mound. The radio echoed over and over "Why aye aye aye, yeah, is Superman dead, aye aye aye, yeah, is it in my head."

"She is funny." My dad chuckled.

"She has been a great support." I commented as I watched the mound.

"What do you plan to do with her when this is all over?" My dad asked.

"Maybe ask her to marry me, when she's old enough." The age thing. It was always there. But in another year it wouldn't matter. Either I'd be dead or she'd be older. At this point the only thing that really mattered was she was keeping me alive.

Leanna bolted out of the woods and jumped back in the car. "I think I saw a moose!"

"Really?" I gave her a sarcastic look.

"Yes!" Leanna smacked my arm.

"Well, this is Rangeley." My dad looked down the road and pulled out.

The day ended with fireworks in Rumford. Leanna and I were both healed that evening. The thundering of explosives, the brilliant flashes of light, there was no darkness for us.

***

"Jason, you are really sick. Your counts are too low to fight off your cold." Doctor K shook his head. "You have cancer. You need to cut this out."

"Cut what out? Living? Yeah, ok Doc." I grinned.

"This isn't funny. You'll be lucky if you don't die this time." He started filling out some papers. "I'm having you admitted today. Right now, Mr. Libby."

Usually I would have fought with Dr. K, but I could hardly breathe. My throat was completely infected. The interior was gross. The whole thing was white and lumpy. There were layers of flesh missing. Red splotches streaked everywhere. I wasn't even able to eat. I had to spit since I couldn't swallow, otherwise I'd fill my lungs full of saliva.

"Ok, Doc. This time I'll go with it. But don't expect me not to have fun while I'm here." I smiled.

I got a room at the far end of the unit. Mercy hospital had been really good to me. I brought my Playstation, a bunch of Godzilla images that I printed from the internet and of course, Leanna. The only stinker about the visit was my throat. I was given a suction tube to put down it. This long piece of plastic tubing was fitted down one side of my mouth. Any liquid that got sucked up was drained into a tub on the wall. The first night I filled it with a combination of blood and saliva. Leanna kept laughing every time it slurped.

***

One night, while Leanna was gone, I had a very unexpected visitor, my Grandpa Libby. Through most of my childhood he had not been in the picture. I am not sure if it was due to family infighting or something else. But not once had he been to see me since I was diagnosed with cancer. He came into the room like a phantom.

"Hey Grandpa." I muttered. The tube in my mouth made it hard for me to speak.

"Hey there, Jason." Grandpa Libby pulled up a chair and sat next to me. He was tall like me and even bald like me. He would have normally shaken my arm out of its socket, but this time he wasn't as hyper. "How are you doing?"

"Well let's see, I have cancer. I am sick as a dog and I'm not getting laid." I smugly replied.

"Oh." He was taken aback by my response. Grandpa Libby was always cheerful, but he was lost at the sight of me.

"What brings you here?" I asked, making sure to suck up a large piece of flem.

"I wanted to see how you were doing." He looked very uncomfortable.

"Well, be it that this is the second time I have had cancer and this is the first time you have come to see me, I'm surprised." I was ruthless. I wanted him to feel what I felt. I wanted him to know that I was going out pissed at him. "How did you find out I was here?"

"Pat called me and told me how bad you were doing." Grandpa looked guilty and Grammy Pat knew how to get the point across.

"Oh, so she called you and gave you grief for not coming to see me sooner?" I really stuck it to him.

"Pretty much." He admitted.

"At least you admit it. For that, I thank you." But it wasn't enough. I drew up as much gross crap as I could and let it slide through the tube. Grandpa Libby looked like he was going to be ill.

"Well I need to go, but I just wanted to check in on you." Grandpa stood up.

I grabbed his hand. Even with all my anger I couldn't just let him walk away. I wanted to tell him I loved him, but I didn't. "Thank you, I mean it." I squeezed his hand tight and then let go. I watched as he walked out the door, in a manner that could only be described as ashamed, but it was I who should have been ashamed and I was. Forgiveness is an important thing. Years later the shoe would be on the other foot. It was important to me to heal the rift when he died from cancer himself. Holding his hand, listening to his confessions, knowing in the end how much he loved us all, but just didn't know how to show it. He died and I wept. This time for a grandfather who I barely got to know, yet had all too much in common with.

Countdown to Death

A week passed after my stay at Mercy. My throat was back to normal. Thank God I was a quick healer. But I was now back at Bethesda and NIH. I sat in the hospital room, alone, scared, and realizing that this was the end. My bed had one of those green mats, the ones for people who crap themselves, throw up on themselves or wet themselves. My heart was already pounding hard. I knew what was coming. A night of pain and suffering, worse than anything I'd experienced so far. I was alone. No one else in my room. For that I was grateful. I was away from the window and the blower. There was an empty bed next to me. It had dead written all over it. Someone had died there. I could feel their pain. My mind was racing. Thinking about my fate. I almost began to panic. I turned the TV on for a distraction, some way to pull my mind from my fate. I started to tear up. I was going to die in this place. So far from home that my body would have to be put on a plane. With my luck, it'd probably crash on the way back to Maine.
"Tonight, an exclusive look at Episode 1." A voice on the TV broke my concentration.
"Sweet!" Like a switch, I forgot about pain, suffering and death and turned my attention to the TV.
A large black lady entered the room. In her hands, a glass bottle and an IV pump. "Mr. Libby, are you ready?"
"Sure, as long as I can catch *ET* tonight." I pointed to the TV and smiled.
"What's on?" She inquired, but I could tell she really didn't care.
"Exclusive scenes from the new Star Wars film."
"Oh." She hung the glass bottle and just barely broke a smile.
I had a feeling. A bad one. One that said if I died, this nurse wouldn't figure it out until the morning. I watched as she attached the IV line to the pump. She smelled like toilet paper or some old lady perfume. I inspected her hair. Extremely curled and so black you might have thought she had a black hole hidden in there.
"Now Mr. Libby, you are going to probably get really sick from this. If you need me just hit your call button and I'll be right in." She smiled.
"What should I be expecting?" Not like I really wanted to know, but I foolishly asked anyway.
"This drug will work into your kidneys. It might burn when you urinate so stay hydrated." She said it in a loving tone, but I knew that she had better things to be doing. She walked towards the door. "Don't for-

get, if you need anything just hit the call button."

I sat there in my bed. Alone. I could feel the poison entering my vein. My nose began to tingle. I laid back and prayed to a God that would not listen to a blasphemous heathen such as myself. I closed my eyes. "Oh God, what have I done?" I kept kidding myself that I would sleep through the whole experience.

***

My wakeup call was not pleasant. It felt as if someone had taken a knife and stabbed me in the stomach, proceeding to then pull at my intestines. My eyes opened in a panic. I looked around. It was still light outside. I looked to the clock hoping for it to be morning. No such luck, an hour had passed. My stomach heaved and I rolled on my side trying to soften the coming blow. Cramping on a level only comparable to childbirth struck me. My vision went blurry and my skin began to turn bright red. I fumbled for the basin on my nightstand. My fingers searched. *Where the fuck is it?* I looked over, it was on the floor. Who the fuck? I hit the nurse call button and reached over the hospital bed railing. It was like a prison bar trying to keep me from my basin. I closed my eyes. *Use the Force.* Nope, the damn thing didn't fly into my hand. Jedi religion based on fact my ass. I made a lunge forward and grasped the basin with my fingers, pulling it up quickly as another wave struck me. My jaw flung open and I proceeded to projectile vomit. Not much hit the basin. It was mostly apple juice that came up. But I still heaved. Dry heaving, bile heaving, die heaving. The pain stopped for a moment. *Where the fuck is my nurse?* I needed help. A larger wave came around and caught me off guard. I cried out in pain. It was worse than having my stomach ripped out. I clenched the call button like I was going to crush it. I hit the button over and over.

"What do you need Mr. Libby?" a voice crackled over a speaker.

"I can't stop throwing…" Another cramp caused me to lose my breath. "Argh!"

"Take a deep breath Mr. Libby. I'll be down in a minute." The voice sounded so detached. I grew angry. *If this is how I was going to be treated I might as well go jump out the window and save myself the grief of suffering.*

I watched the clock between cramp waves. My basin was filling up quickly. Foaming bile slithered across the liquid juices that had been making a lake. Two minutes passed, vomit. Four minutes passed, cramping and vomit. Eight minutes passed, I blacked out. Fifteen minutes later

I awoke to more cramping and I was lying in a puddle of vomit. I sat up and began to cry. My dignity was taking a pounding. Finally, twenty minutes later, the nurse came in.

"Looks like we had a little accident here." She turned around and walked out.

"Really, you think?" I raised my voice. "What took you so long?"

"I was with another patient." She yelled from down the hall.

"Well you could have told me that instead of making me wait this long." I was so pissed I could have hit her with a goddamn chair. The smell of bile penetrated my nose. I climbed out of my bed and staggered to the bathroom, IV pole in tow. It was a large bathroom, much larger than any hospital bathroom I had seen before. It had a large sink area, a nice toilet and a large shower. I grabbed a white towel that was hanging on the wall. The black NIH stenciling was appealing. I washed up.

"Would you like to see if I can get you some morphine?" The nurse peeked her head in.

"That shit makes me sick. Do you have anything else?" I stopped what I was doing, my stomach began to cramp. "All I want to be able to do is eat a little and go to sleep."

"We have the pot pill." She smiled. Maybe because she had taken some or maybe because she knew it might work.

"Pot pill?" It sounded interesting.

"It's in clinicals right now. It's an opium extract. It works really fast." Her head disappeared.

"Let me make a quick phone call and I'll let you know." I was still in the Navy. Drugs were against regulation, pot especially. I went into my small drawer and pulled out my wallet. I set down my phone card and my USNR command numbers. Sitting down on my bed I dialed Chief Johnson. The phone rang.

"HTC Johnson, Naval Reserve Center Portland." His voice was soothing to me. A comfort that I needed at that moment.

"Chief, it's me Libby." My voice started to get hoarse.

"Lib, what's happening?" He sounded happy to hear from me.

"I'm pretty sick. I am calling to ask permission to take a drug that is an opium extract. I'll pop a piss test if I take it." The last thing I wanted to do was get busted for pot while I was in the Navy.

"Damn, Lib. You don't need to ask me permission. If it will help you feel better you'd better well take it." Like the father figure he always was, Chief was protective of me.

"Aye, aye. Thank you, Chief." I started to cry. I was living this nightmare and still my shipmates treated me like a real person.

"No problem. Just get better so I can put you back to work." Chief Johnson hung up the phone.

The nurse came back in. "So?"

"I'll try it." I rested my head against a fresh pillow and closed my eyes.

Instead of an eternity for the nurse to get back to me, she came in ten minutes later with two pills. "Mr. Libby, dinner is in thirty minutes. I'll give you these pills now so you'll be able to eat your meal while it's hot."

The pills were green gel caps. Inside, opium. I wasn't a stranger to pot. I had smoked it once after the first time I had cancer. I ended up staring up at a ceiling the whole night that time. "Thank you."

I popped the pills into my mouth and dry swallowed them. The nurse made a disgusted face and walked out.

***

I was lucky enough not to vomit after taking the pills. The 'munchy' effect kicked in within five minutes. I sat patiently and waited for dinner, my stomach begging for food, which is pretty damn funny considering that only a handful of minutes ago I was ready to just die.

"Mr. Libby," a woman peeked her head into my room, "I have your dinner."

"Sweet!" I sat up in my bed and scoped out the tray.

"There isn't much here because they said you were really sick." The woman was cute, in her colorful clothes, hard Middle Eastern accent, and those beautiful eyes.

I found myself mesmerized by her. My jaw must have been just hanging there. I almost slipped and asked her if she was interested in giving a dying man one last good time. Then I thought back to Leanna and I switched my hormones off. "I am starved, so any food is good food."

She placed the tray on my table and moved it into position so I could eat. I could smell her hair through my metallic nostrils. Spices. Beautiful spices. I allowed the scent to travel into my stomach, where I mentally devoured her. "Is there anything else you need?"

There was: Just her company. Her smell. Her eyes. Her flesh. I shook my head. "No, thank you. But thank you for making my day." I winked at her and she broke a half smile, leaving me sitting there. Alone. Utterly alone.

The tray had the basics. Jell-o, a breaded dish and juice. I gazed at the apple juice. "Fucking thing. I had better not puke you up again." I took my fork and dove into my breaded meal. The first bite was the test. Would I throw up? Would I become so deathly ill that I'd die? Oh, fuck, who the hell cares, I had the munchies! It was like heaven. Before I knew it I had consumed everything on the plate. My stomach begged for more. I slurped the Jell-o, but it still didn't fill me. I guzzled the juice. My stomach growled more.

"Mr. Libby, how was your meal?" My nurse asked as she entered the room. "My goodness, you were hungry!"

"Munchies. I need more." My stomach let out a nasty growl.

"You want to be careful, the pill helps you eat, but you still could get sick." She acted all concerned.

"At least can you bring me some bread and crackers?" I begged. My stomach was cramping from my damn pot induced hunger.

"I'll be back in a minute." There it was again. Be back in a minute. Would it be hours this time? It didn't matter too much because I wasn't puking myself to death, I was simply hungry. But she was back before I could contemplate how I was going to get out of bed and get the rations myself.

"Thank you." I smiled and then dove into the food. The crackers didn't last long at all.

***

I watched the clock waiting for *Entertainment Tonight* to come on. I had something to be excited about *Star Wars Episode 1* clips were just the pill this doctor ordered. At the three minute mark something began to happen. My stomach gurgled a nasty tune. It wasn't cramping, at least not at first. More like every liquid I had drank began rushing through my intestines. Oh wonderful, diarrhea. I pushed the hospital table to one side and started to get up. Then like a hammer striking a tin wall I convulsed backwards. It felt like a seizure. My body thrashed for a moment out of control and I cried out in pain as my insides felt like they had been torn out. As my head rebounded off the bed my dinner sprayed out of my mouth, a mixture of dark bile and food. At the same time my intestines gave way. I felt the warmth of body waste run into my hospital clothes. I struggled to get up and to the bathroom, but I had no control over my body. A constant wave of pain shot through me and at both ends everything in me evacuated. The smell of vomit and diarrhea was overwhelming. I fell onto the floor and smacked the nurse call button. Crawling to the bathroom was difficult. I was soaked in the most disgusting materials from the human body. I managed to grab a towel from the nightstand and use it to keep anymore fluids from getting onto anything. Pulling together what strength I could, I rushed into the bathroom and slammed the door, the IV pole almost falling over when it hit the bathroom tile. I quickly stripped naked, being careful not to blow my IV. The shower spit out warm water and I climbed inside. The body wastes washed away. I began to cry. All I wanted to fucking do is watch that one damn Star Wars segment, but no, now I was stuck in the bathroom.

Once my skin smelled clean, I went and opened the bathroom door. I could hear the Star Wars segment starting. My stomach cramped and I could feel my intestines filling up. Quickly I sat on the toilet and a constant stream poured out of me. It felt like I was pissing out of my ass. Then came the voice. Yoda, Liam Neeson and the music of Star Wars. I tried to lift myself up, but my stomach heaved. My hand was able to retrieve the bathroom trashcan just as bile exploded from my mouth and more water from my ass. *You've got to be kidding me...* I listened from the bathroom as the Star Wars segment continued on without me. Just as it was about to end my stomach stopped doing whatever the hell it was doing. I jumped up and ran to the TV. All I had time to see was a domed hut on what looked like Tatooine. Yippie skippie. My bed was a mess. Vomit and diarrhea sat in the middle of it like a lake. Still no nurse. I reached down and picked up the call button and pushed it again. All I had on me was a white towel across my waist, my wasted little waist. I gathered up my sheets and cleaned up my mess.

"Mr. Libby, did you call?" My nurse entered the room.

"I was really sick." I continued to clean.

"Smells like it. Take a seat, sweety and I'll get you some new pajamas." The nurse left the room.

She returned with an armload of bedding and some fresh pajamas. "You know, when you start feeling sick like that you should head to the bathroom right away and hit your call button."

I looked at her for a moment, almost cursed out loud and then just nodded my head. "Yep."

"Did you get to see your Star Wars?" She asked.

"No, I could only hear it from the bathroom." I scowled at her. She bent over in front of me, her ass was huge. Well maybe not huge, but big. As Sergio used to say "I love those big ole' white butts on those white girls." But this chick was black. I pondered the logic in what Sergio had said, but it just brought me back to the whole 'white meat/dark meat' discussion. Hadn't had dark meat before. I chuckled.

"What's so funny?" The nurse turned around.

"Nothing, just thinking of better times." I lied through my teeth. I was curious about interracial dating. But I also had Leanna waiting for me at home. Conflict filled my brain. I retrieved my wallet and pulled out my calling card. I watched as the nurse finished making my bed.

***

I had waited for the perfect time to call Leanna. I hadn't talked to her since I checked into NIH. My stomach was settled for now. The phone rang, digital tone, technological music, it was all a sign of the times.

"Hello?" It was her. Leanna's voice. Almost like a euphoric sound.

"Hey, Chicky Monkey." I kept my voice to the typical Jay tone, not letting her on to how sick I was this time.

"Hey, Gummi! I miss you!" She perked up and excitement filled her voice.

"I miss you too. I just wanted to check in before I go to bed." My stomach began to turn.

"I'm glad you did. So how is it this time?"

"I'm ok. A little sicker than usual, but I'm Jay. You can't keep a good god down." I laughed.

"Yep, typical. You must be feeling ok."

The cramping began. I had to make it quick. "I hate to cut this short, but I need to get another shot."

"So, talk to me while they stick you. It'll be like holding your hand." She was buying time. Time I didn't have.

"I really need to go. I am sorry." My head began to spin frantically. It was coming. "I love you."

She began to speak the words "I love you" but I was halfway to hanging up. The pain was much more intense than last time. I struggled once again to get up, but it was too late. My stomach exploded at both ends. I blacked out, waking up moments later in a bed with a lake of vomit and diarrhea. I was soaked. My head spun out of control. Small amounts of bile made their way out of my mouth as I fell onto the floor, almost taking the IV poll with me. *Got to reach the bathroom.* I kept telling myself that. Inch by inch, mile by mile, hour by hour, time and distance were irrelevant. Getting to my feet was a major task. I was in an abyss. A place of nothingness. I started to blank out. I remember the shower water running over my tainted flesh. Foam at my feet from the bile and intestinal content. No odor at all. What was coming out of me was just me. Nothing more. The toilet made a good throne. I sat there.

My ass burned as chemicals scorched me. There was no kidney damage going on here. My intestines and butt were taking the brunt of this whole damn thing. It hurt to wipe myself.

"Mr. Libby!" a voice broke my concentration. "What the hell happened here?!"

"I, I…" no memory….. "I got sick?"

"I guess you did! How did you get out of bed?" She scorned me.

No memory. I tried to think back. But like a chalkboard being erased, I was slowly losing everything. "I got up and came in…"

"Well at least you are cleaned up. I'll get you new sheets and pajamas, again." She sounded a little upset.

I was clean. I tried to picture my grandfather in my head. An anchor to my past. The one thing that might be able to hold me together. But I could only picture him in one scene. One piece. One penny.

In my dress blues. Coming home on leave. The last time I saw him. He was sitting there in his yellow leather chair. Listening to one of his talking books. He didn't know I was coming. Charles Parker was many things to me. Most of all he was the relative I loved more than anyone else. His opinion was the only one that ever mattered. He was my anchor to order. I popped onto the porch.

"Grandpa!"

His eyes lit up. I had seen him happy before, but nothing like this. His physical limitation vanished. Without his walker, without his cane, Charles F. Parker stood up on his own and walked to me. He embraced me like I was a long lost son. He did not let go of me. I hugged him back. My only true role model in life besides the characters from G.I. Joe. But Grandpa was real. A real person. "JP!"

That was it. That was all I had at that moment. Just him hugging me and calling me "JP." I held in my pain. My sorrow over his loss. His death. It was inevitable that he would die first. The nurse placed new pajamas on the sink. I smiled a fake smile and she left. I began to whimper like a little child. I was alone. Again. And now the only past I had for sure was the memory of a dead man, making me even more miserable. I looked up to the ceiling. "Fuck you, God, fuck you."

***

I awoke the next morning to my mother's voice. She sounded happy as could be. "Wake up. Time to go."

My head was still spinning from the ordeal. "Yeah, I know. Let's get the hell out of here." I tried to climb out of bed, but found my legs weren't working too well. I couldn't walk. I attempted to place pressure on them, but they would not support my weight. "This isn't good."

"Here, let me help you." My mother retrieved my clothes and proceeded to assist me in getting dressed. If she had her good moments, this was one of them. Lucky for me she was a RN. One leg at a time I slid into my pants. I was able to get my shirt on by myself.

A knock at the door. Karen came in. My South American nurse from the Outpatient clinic was a sight for sore eyes. "I heard you didn't do too well last night. I've brought you your syringes and a wheelchair. You'll need to go to the pharmacy down stairs for your drugs."

"Cool." My mother propped me up and helped me to the wheelchair outside the room. I hated wheelchairs. They made me feel like a cripple. But I was, wasn't I? I had lost most of the use of my legs. Who was I to complain about this? People live with this shit everyday.

"Please be careful, Jason." Karen bent down and gave me a hug. Her petite little form was easy to grasp. "This is the one time where you could die if you are not careful."

"I'm Jay, I don't die."

"Oh, here we go again. Youthful God complex." My mother rolled her eyes and tossed my syringes in my black leather bag. The rough leather scuffed by pale flesh.

"You won't be saying that when I walk out of Mercy." I chuckled in a snide way.

"Jason, you are so crazy." Karen patted my bald head. "Sharon, can I talk with you a second?"

My mother and Karen vanished. I couldn't hear what they were saying. I could barely keep my head upright. I felt extremely ill, but nothing like the death pains from overnight. I looked down the hallway. The denizens of cancer hell wandered. Children, women, men, all sick, all dying. And here I was. On my way out. Out into the real world of the living. I was not dead. Not yet.

***

The Reagan Jetport was crowded. People scurrying along to their flights. I sat in a wheelchair, hunched over, hiding myself behind my black leather bag, clenching it like it was my life. It was. Inside over $30,000 worth of Neupogen and needles. Enough supplies to get me through a couple of weeks. My mother wheeled me over to the metal detectors.

"Can he stand up?" a male security guard asked.

"I doubt it. He just finished a really high dose of chemo." My mother responded carefully.

"Got any bombs in there?" The man reached for the bag.

"Yeah, I am really going to blow up a plane. Dude, I'm in the Navy." I pulled out my ID and tried cramming it into his face.

"Doesn't matter. I need to check the bag." He snapped back.

"Well we need to do this somewhere less in the open." My mother shook her head.

"Don't ask me to strip." I scowled at the guard.

The security guard made my mother walk next to me while he pushed me. A female officer followed us into a private room. They took the bag from me and dropped it on a table.

"Careful!" My mother tried to soften the impact, but the female officer stopped her.

The bag was opened carefully, like there might really be a bomb inside. My syringes and cooler bags were dumped out. "Holy shit." The female officer went for her radio.

"Easy there. It's for my meds. A shot every morning in the stomach. Without them I could end up deader than I already am." I winked at the woman.

"Sorry for the holdup." The male stuffed everything back in my bag and handed it to me carefully. "I'll personally take you to your plane."

I felt like a VIP. People cleared the path to the plane and I was surrounded by security. My mother and I were the first to be seated. The walk onto the plane was hard. My legs felt so weak. Each step felt as if I was falling off a cliff. My mother held me tight as I went seat to seat, trying to find our number so I could collapse. Once we were seated I lost touch with reality. It felt like I might die.

Of course, when the plane took off I came around. I gripped the arm rest like I was going to crash and panicked as my connection with the Earth abandoned me.

"Are you ok?" My mother held my hand in a way that a mother would when her child is going to die.

"I just want to go home." I whispered.

"We're on the way there."

***

Two days after I returned from NIH.

"What's up?" Leanna approached me in my blind spot.

"Packing." I feverishly stuffed a folder with Godzilla prints.

"Is it that time already?" Leanna sat down on the futon and

watched.

My heart paused. It was that time. I no sooner got home than my counts were already hitting below safe. I had gotten almost no time with Leanna outside of the hospital.

"I'm really going to be sick this time." I could barely look into her eyes. She made me melt in some way. Maybe it was her innocence, or the lack of it. But Leanna had a quality to her that I could not draw myself away from.

"Well I'm here for you Gummi." She jumped up, all spirited and gave me one of her soft hugs. I kissed Leanna on the lips. It was a kiss long overdue. She sat on my lap and moved herself for a better angle. Our lips kept pressing, I could feel her tongue trying to break my cautious barrier, and finally I let my desires take control. In my life, I had never felt so much passion behind a kiss. It was like it would be the last one. After this I would be gone forever. Leanna must have felt that way too. A passion out of control and a surrender that took her someplace that she had never been with a man. All I could do was offer her release, and our hearts became intertwined in a way that I couldn't explain. So much I had denied myself, yet in my last hours I could not let her not know me.

An hour passed and we sat on the futon, wrapped in a blanket, snuggled up together, still kissing. "I don't want to lose you." Leanna gripped my hand and kissed me again.

"I'm Jay." I laughed a fake laugh.

"I know, and you don't die." Leanna climbed on me and let herself be exposed.

"Well I don't." I wiggled my hips and rubbed against her. "Fear is the mind killer, and I do not fear." I lied. Reality was beginning to set in. The event that I had just enjoyed was probably my last.

I rolled Leanna off of me, winked and then stood up. My body scrawny and ghost white, but covered in sweat. "I'm inspired."

"For what?" Leanna asked.

"Road trip!" I clapped my hands and tossed Leanna her shorts.

"Are you sure you will be ok to do it?" Leanna sat up, her breasts glistening in the sunlight.

"Fuck'n A right!" I was quick to get dressed. Throwing on essentials along with some cologne to mask the sweet smell of Leanna.

The Guyver, my little red Mazda, loved a good road trip. Not telling Leanna where we were going, I plotted a course for New Hampshire. The music was simple to choose for this drive. 3rd Eye Blind the whole way. Leanna and I chanted the chorus to *Semi-Charmed Life*, a song we knew all too well.

"I'm not listening when you say" I sang at the top of my lungs.

"Goodbye, goodbye eye eye, goodbyeeeee!" Leanna laughed and our hands clapped together like we had just scored a killer shot in basketball.

"We make a killer team." Happiness ruled over me at that moment.

"Yes we do, Gummi." Leanna snatched my hand off the stick shift and gave it a vacuum kiss. "I don't want this to end. I'll love you forever and ever and ever, to infinity and beyond."

Forever. It wasn't going to be forever. The words rolled off her lips, but I wasn't going to live forever. I wasn't going to live past the end of the month. I felt a cold chill behind my neck. A tingling. A haunting feeling that I was about to get royally screwed in the game of life. My mind began to lose touch with the world.

"Jay?"

I could see myself laying in bed. Lifeless. Cold and grey. Alone.

"Jay…"

My heart began to pound harder and harder.

"Jesus. Jay!" There was a smacking of skin on skin as Leanna's hand struck my face and just in time.

I reacted quickly as the Guyver almost took a spill into a ditch. Making sure not to overcorrect I steered up onto the soft dirt and stopped the car. My hands were covered in sweat.

"Are you ok?" Leanna turned my head towards her. "Are you with me?"

"Yeah, I think." I looked into her eyes. The next song was blasting on the CD player.

"Do you want me to drive?" Her eyes were bulging and her skin bright red. A panic stricken look.

"Funny, Monkey. I'm ok to drive." I turned down the radio and pulled back onto the road. "Bananas in pajamas are coming after you…." I laughed, Leanna kept staring at me. Like she was trying to make sure it was all ok. Her hand reached around my wrist and we continued on. Her fingers pressing into my vein. She was getting smart. Too smart. She was monitoring my pulse. I underestimated her.

***

Thirty minutes into New Hampshire we pulled into a campground with a store out front. The brown, busted up wooden sign read: Last Stop. The store itself was an old cabin that was reworked to house a small convenience store. The logs on the outside were splintered and looked like they might have an army of ants living inside. The front door was this white metal thing with a screen. It was propped open, as was the wooden door that kept people from just walking in at night. Leanna looked at me funny. Behind the store were dozens of old cabins. I turned onto the road. Down the street were the White Mountains. The titan-like peaks reaching above the tree line in the distance. "The Gods await me." The pine trees on both sides of the road created a throne room appearance. A simple sign read "Kangamangus Highway."

"Are we going in?" Leanna broke my concentration.

"Yep. Let's get some grub before we hit the Kangamangus!" I pivoted on my right heel and marched into the store.

The inside was more amazing than the outside. Leanna looked like she was going to gag. Twinky packages, covered in dust, that almost looked like they had been there since the seventies. Even the simple design on the package screamed seventies. The soda bottles in the cooler. Seventies. The beef jerky packages. Seventies. The bloody roadmap. Seventies.

"Ok, I feel like I just went through a time warp." Leanna giggled.

"This reminds me of the TARDIS." I did a quick spot check for any aliens moping around. "Bigger on the inside than the outside." And that was no lie. The cabin was truly bigger on the inside than out. Or they just knew exactly how to make use of the space. An older woman sat at the counter. Seventies.

"I'm going to grab a tuna sandwich." Leanna opened up a refrigerator and pulled from it a neatly wrapped, white bread lunch.

I scoped the menu posted behind the old lady. Chili dogs. I smiled. "I'll take a chili dog, please."

The woman smiled, her fake white teeth almost looked out of place. I watched as she placed a wrinkled hotdog into a fresh roll. She then picked up a seventies style spoon and started scooping brownish chili from a container. The beans looked as if they'd been sitting there....since the seventies. A grin formed on my face. I could feel Leanna's disgusted look behind me, piercing my form and analyzing the material going into my lunch.

"Monkey, grab some Yoohoo, please." Yoohoo was my drink of choice. It had some healthy things to it, but I couldn't tell you what.

Leanna returned with two bottles. Seventies. There was a nice layer of dust on them. Leanna gave me a look. That look of "Let's get the fuck out of here." Her eyes rolled as the seventy year old lady rang us up.

"Have a nice day." I heard the woman mumble as we ran out the door.

"You too!" Leanna and I both shouted.

We jumped into the Guyver and took off, leaving a massive cloud of dust behind us.

Two big bites. That's all it took. The chili dog was gone. Leanna was taking her time with her sandwich. Simple bites. But for me, no, I ate it in two big bites.

"I guess you were hungry." Leanna giggled.

"Well considering this might be one of my last meals, I'll take it." I made a fist, causing the napkin to crumple up, the chili stains almost looked like blood. I snapped my forearm back and the napkin hit the floor.

"As long as you have me, you'll be fine." Her voice was reassuring. But it wasn't the truth. I knew it. I was going to die. No matter how many barriers I tossed up I was going to kick it. And this girl, this sweet girl was going be the one getting hurt. Leanna kissed my cheek, tuna falling onto the emergency brake handle. She was quick to clean it up. I looked at her. Her breasts, her cheeks, her lips, her hair, her eyes. We looked at one another.

"I love you." I smiled. I did. I loved her more than she could imagine.

"I do too. Love you." Leanna's eyes sparkled.

The last stretch of the Kangamangus was fun. Curvy roads, rivers, mountains, lots of ups and downs. My stomach was beginning to quiver. "We need to pull over." The cramping hit me out of nowhere. Oh shit, not here. Not now. Not in front of her.

"Are you ok?" Leanna grabbed my wrist again.

"Starting to feel sick. Let's pull over." My driving was precise. The Guyver turned sharply into a rest stop at the last second. No sooner did I slam on the breaks I opened the door and fell out.

"Jay!" Leanna screamed and ran to join me.

My hands were buried in the dirt and rocks. Flies buzzed around me. The trees swayed from the mountain breeze. My stomach twisted and I cried out. "Get BACK!" I screamed. Leanna stopped in her tracks. I could feel the build up. I knew what was coming.

"Let me help!" Leanna tried to step forward.

"Get BACK!" I cried out. Struggling to my feet I turned away from the Guyver. My stomach emptied onto the ground. Everything.

"Jesus Jay," Leanna laughed, "Did you even chew that thing?"

I looked down. Two whole pieces of hotdog floating in a pool of

Yoohoo and chili. I looked at Leanna. She was standing there smiling. The smile. One of happiness. I smiled back.

"Teaches you to chew your food." Leanna scolded me.

I broke into laughter. It was a release. We both stood there and laughed. Then hugged. Then I fell onto the ground, the world spinning out of control.

"Jay?" Leanna pulled me up, putting my arm over her shoulder.

"You need to drive. I can't do it. Everything is so fucked up." I couldn't get it under control. The spinning was making me sicker.

"I gotchya, Gummi." Leanna was tough. She helped me to the passenger seat of the Guyver and set me down carefully. I could feel her hands across my stomach as she quickly buckled me.

"Take me to Mercy." I cried. And I cried some more. I was no longer in control. But Leanna was good at keeping secrets. She held my hand tight.

"Are you sure?" She asked.

"I need to get my central line in before I get admitted." I closed my eyes. Darkness. Nothingness. Chaos.

***

The penetration, the tickle, the rush. "There you go Mr. Libby." Dr. K rubbed his gloved hands together. "All done."

"Thanks, Doc." I sat up in bed. Leanna, a CNA and two nurses watched. I recognized the CNA as the one who had been with me from the start. Only now was I taking the time to really look at her. Curly blonde hair, glasses, a cute form and wrinkled skin, but not old.

"I want to introduce you to Dawn and Kate." Dr. K was pointing to the nurses. I had met Kate once before in passing. She was in her thirties, or at least looked it. She had a full head of brown hair that was pulled back so it would not infringe on her duties as a nurse. Dawn was totally different. She had that eighties hair thing going, with a slender form to die for and a cute face. "They will be following your case for me when I am not around."

"Nice to meet you, Mr. Libby." Kate's voice was working class Brit.

"Nice to meet you, too." I smiled. Leanna gave me a jealous look. "But we can cut the formalities. Call me Jay."

"Well, Jay, it is nice to meet you." Dawn stepped up and gave me a huge smile. Her hand reached out and when I shook it, I dwarfed her tiny digits. "I'll come to check on you during the day. I'm the outpatient

Oncology nurse."

"I'll be seeing you in the evenings and on weekends." Kate waved.

"Thank you." I watched as my two newest friends left the room. "Cute nurses." I winked at Leanna.

"Be nice to them. They will be taking care of you specifically." Dr. K pulled my chart to his chest and started writing. "You can go home to pack. I'll see you probably tomorrow."

"Sure, Doc. I bet I'll be fine until the weekend is over." I laughed. Dr. K did not.

"Young lady." He turned to Leanna. "Get him back here tomorrow or else."

"Don't worry Doctor K. I'll drag him in kicking and screaming if I have to." Leanna's face got tight, her cheeks raised and she stared at me in a very mean way. As if to say that I WOULD follow Doctor K's orders.

***

So the next day....

Moving into a hospital isolation room is a very precise thing. Especially one where there are two doors to keep people and germs out. Sister Mary watched as I brought two giant duffle bags into my hospital room. Leanna was right behind me with a box. Godzilla images, again. The Playstation, again. More controllers. More games. Thumbtacks. And of course, me.

"Looks like you are all ready to go." Sister Mary laughed as she straightened a crooked image of Godzilla on my bulletin board.

"Moving in?" my regular CNA marched into the room with an armload of hospital gowns.

"What's your name?" I asked.

"Kathy." My head was already having trouble remembering names. Kate, Kathy, Dawn. Although Dawn I could remember well enough because of my ex. Same name, totally different bodies.

***

"Jason." I looked through the ceiling. Just lying there. Looking through the plaster, wires and tile. The voice was part of the illusion. "Jason we need to move you."

I blinked, turned my head and saw Kathy standing there. "I just moved in two days ago."

"We have a Tuberculosis patient coming onto the unit and we

need this room to isolate him." Kathy started packing up my stuff. Thumbtacks dropped into a plastic cup. Papers stacked upon one another.

"What the fuck do you mean I need to move? I am vulnerable to any germ!" I raised my voice and sat all the way up. My head began to spin out of control and I fell back.

"We're moving you to the end of the hall to a private room. Don't worry." Kathy walked out of my room and came back in with a small cart. The wheels on the cart screeched along the waxed floor. On the cart was one of those white face masks. The ones you see surgeons wear. Like a disk thrower, Kathy flicked her wrist and the mask landed on my lap. "Suit up. We're going."

NIH always said that those masks were bad for you. Especially when you were neutropenic. They used to say that bacteria and germs could build up on the mask and actually make you sick. Yet, there I sat with one in my lap. Choices. A lot of choices.

"Jason put the mask on." Kathy walked over to me and put the mask over my face. She then grabbed my central line like a leash and tugged. "Get up."

"Oh now that's cheating." The thing about a central line is it's actually stitched into your skin. That way it doesn't accidentally come out. There was a small pain in my neck as she tugged and I quickly got myself out of bed.

"There we go." Kathy giggled a little.

Another nurse appeared in the doorway. I saw her feet first and then those perfect legs. As my head scoped upwards I saw a perfect waist, stomach, a beautiful chest, the face of a goddess and then bright blonde hair. "Is he ready?" Her voice was lotion on my chafed spirit.

"All set here." I snatched my line out of Kathy's hand and stood upright, in order to not look like a hunchback and grabbed my IV pole. There was no name for this nurse of absolute beauty.

"Oh, so I see you'll do it for the Blonde Bombshell." Kathy barked at me and retrieved my cart loaded full of personal items.

"It's all in how you ask." I winked at Kathy and puckered my lips through the white surgical mask.

As we walked past this beautiful newcomer, I heard her whisper to Kathy "Blonde Bombshell?"

"Sweety, you are absolutely gorgeous." Kathy whispered back.

"But in front of a patient?" I moved forward and put the ladies behind me.

"His dad was the old head nurse here. He's practically family." I heard Kathy defend herself.

The walk to my new room, my death room, was long. While only down to the end of the hallway, it was still a long haul. I looked into other rooms as I labored to my resting place. Old people. Young people. Dying people. Family members crying. Family members laughing. The overhead pages. The beeping of IV pumps. The screeching of the wheels on the cart. The clicking of shoes from the women behind me. Clicking. Like a gun out of ammo. Aimed at my head. Waiting for me to hit the loaded chamber. Waiting for me to die.

The long walk ended. I peeked into my final resting place. Empty, with just a TV leaning out from the wall at the foot of a very old looking hospital bed. I say old because unlike my other beds, this one was less high tech. A death bed. A bed that people die on. There was a window, looking out to a brick wall. No view. Just the death view. The view one has before they die, when your life comes to a screeching halt. I chuckled.

"So this is it, huh?" I looked back at the two women behind me.

"At least it's quiet down here. You'll have some peace." The Blonde Bombshell smiled. I knew she meant well, but it didn't help.

I walked into the room and pointed to the wall by the window. "You can leave the cart here."

"Do you want us to help you unpack?" Kathy asked in a very tender voice. The type of voice you use on a child, or someone who was about to die.

"I've got it. Besides, Leanna will be here in a few. She can decorate it for me." A few, more like an hour. An eternity. But I had my Playstation so it wasn't like I was stuck watching dry VH1 programming. Dave Mathews and Hansen videos had become all too common.

"Well if you need anything, call." Kathy waved and the Blond Bombshell followed her out the door.

"Let's get busy." I quickly pulled my Playstation from the pile on the cart and untangled wires. I reached up behind the looming TV and disconnected the back, inserting my Playstation connector and reattaching the wiring. I had a small stack of games. I fumbled through the pile and found the game. THE GAME. Wing Commander IV. I had just bought it before I had checked myself into the hospital. This game had movies, famous actors like Malcolm McDowell, giving you the urge to kill them on sight, and some of the best space fighter action to ever grace my military hands. I had even purchased a special joystick controller so I could keep the feel real. I had time. Leanna's welcome visit was still a bit off. It was time to kill some kitties.

***

Time flies when you are having fun. Days fly by, you forget that you are going to die, and when the nurses aren't looking you are sneaking some fun time in with the one you love. I was living the life in a hospital room. The reality of cancer had fallen to the wayside and I was happy.

"Jason." Dawn came into my room, all smiles, with Kate right behind her.

"Well if it isn't my two favorite nurses." I pushed pause on my controller, allowing my pilot to actually get a rest. "What can I do for you?"

"Well." Dawn sat down in the chair that had been brought into my room for Leanna. A chair that had seen much use in the week I had been there. "We have this patient that has cancer. He is really being a pain in the ass to the nursing staff. His attitude is going to kill him."

"We were wondering if you could go across the hall and explain to him why he needs to cooperate for us." Kate's English accent was hot. But at the same time I didn't get all hormonal over her. Instead it soothed me.

"What? Am I the new poster child for cancer patients?" I laughed.

"Your cancer is far worse than his." Dawn patted my knee. "He needs a wakeup call."

"Sure, why not?" I uncovered myself while Dawn prepped an IV poll for my hydration bag.

The walk across the hallway was simple. I looked down to where the nurse's station was. The staffers were busy doing their own things. As I reached the door, Dawn whispered to me. "His name is Peter."

"Gotchya." I winked.

Peter's room had two beds, separated by a curtain. The bed I was directed to was occupied by a guy with all his hair and a mustache. He looked like a biker. He wasn't too old, his hair only had a slight sign of gray mixed with the jet black strands. Peter looked at me. I could see anger in him. A lot of anger.

"Who are you?" He barked at me. "Wait, let me guess, the nurses sent you in here to make me feel bad for not taking my pills."

"For one, lose the fucking attitude." I snapped at him. Dawn was hiding in the hallway and broke out a giggle. "I am here because I care enough to be."

"So what do you have?" Peter toned down his voice.

"Non-Hodgkin's Large Cell Lymphoma." I replied, keeping my voice hard, not to show any weakness.

"So do I." Peter sat up in his bed a little and his cheeks went from tight to loose.

"Good. Then we are on the same page." I rolled my IV poll to the foot of his bed.

"Is that what I am going to look like after I have more chemo." Peter didn't even have the chemo colored paste skin. But he wouldn't look like me.

"Depends."

"Depends on what?"

"Depends on if you live to go as far as I have."

"What's that mean?"

"It means if you keep acting like a baby you aren't going to make it. People have cancer a hell of a lot worse than what we have. Those people are going to fucking die. You and I. Well, we are damn lucky that we have nurses like Dawn to keep us going." I pointed my finger at him and started yelling. "Seriously. What the fuck is your malfunction? Don't you want to live? Don't you want to see your kids grow up? Dawn, get in here!"

Dawn came in the door. Her face was bright red. Kate followed. The two had signs of hard laughing. "Yes?" Dawn was struggling not to laugh.

"What is Peter here having such a hard time doing?" The room began to spin a little.

"Prednisone." Dawn replied and Peter scowled at her.

"Jesus Christ!" I turned to Peter. He was all but a blur. "Put it in some fucking ice cream and stop acting like such a baby! And when we get the hell out of here the first round of drinks are on me!"

"You heard him, Peter." Dawn grabbed my shoulder as I tilted.

"You can beat this. I know you can." I had no energy left in me. My voice was soft. The anger gone from it. "I'll be across the hallway if you need someone to talk to." I staggered from the room. Dawn holding me upright.

"Who was that?" I heard Peter ask.

"That's someone who has cancer worse than you and he's probably going to die. He just wanted to make sure you didn't give up." Kate whispered.

I may have been dying, but I wasn't deaf. What Kate said was true. I knew the odds were stacked against me. But I was determined to live and there wasn't anything that was going to stop me. Dawn helped me into bed.

"Thank you, Jason." Dawn smiled.

"Not a problem. I hope I didn't go overboard on him." I rested my head on my hospital pillow.

"He needed it." Dawn's hand rubbed my arm and she walked out of the room.

I had forgotten about the outside world. I had been lost in Wing Commander and Leanna. Both were addictive, but only one I really loved. I closed my eyes knowing that Leanna would be the person to wake me.

***

Soft lips. Soft skin. Soft smell. "Hey, Gummi." The voice whispered in my ear. The soft angelic voice of Leanna.

"Hey, Sea Monkey." I reached up and pulled her close for another kiss. "How was the game?"

Covered in dust from the ball field and still in her red and white uniform, Leanna sat next to me and smiled. "We kicked some serious butt."

"Congrats."

"So what did you do today besides kill kitties all day?" Leanna pulled a tissue from the nearby bland colored tissue box.

"I went and talked to another cancer patient who was acting like a baby over prednisone." I smiled. All the stress from the day was vanishing like a droplet of water off of a hot surface. Leanna did that for me.

"How did that go?"

"I used the "F" word a couple times." I shrugged.

"Gummi!" She slapped my arm. The impact was weak. She knew better than to hit me too hard.

I pointed to the table with the Playstation games. "Grab Tekken 2, Sea Monkey. Time for me to kick your ass."

"Bring it, Gummi." Leanna jumped up and loaded the game.

Between punching, kicking, and the occasional taunt, I couldn't help but to look at Leanna. Here was this girl, this young girl. Well maybe not that young, but still young enough. And she was sitting here with me. Keeping me company. Making sure I was not alone. She had come a long way from the party girl who thought that drinking and having sex were the two coolest things to live for. Now she was more mature. Maybe too mature. Leanna had joined my life at the end of it. She knew how bad it was. Yet she still stayed by my side. She was making me live when no one else would. Even my closest friends had backed away. Only Jay dared come to my room once a week. Leanna was there every day. Her eyes were so beautiful. Her skin so soft. Her fists, so badass. This was not some weak girl. This girl was a hard working, dedicated bad motha. And she was mine.

Leanna's character from Tekken 2 fell to the ground. She turned to see I wasn't even watching the game, I was watching her. "How long have you been looking at me?" Leanna's face was beet red. Angry red.

"Long enough to know that I love you and I always will. Forever and ever." I reached for her hand. Her hand that was still covered in dust, sweat and god knows what else.

"I ought to kick your ass for beating me like that." Leanna stood up and dropped the controller on my bed. She made two fists and put up her dukes.

I rolled over exposing a bare white cheek. "I'm waiting, Sea Monkey."

"Cute butt. No point in messing it up." Leanna kissed her hand and gave my pasty flesh a love tap. She then leaned over me. Her blond hair rolled off her shoulders. Her eyes met mine and she rubbed her nose against my nose. "I love you, too. Forever and ever and into infinity and beyond." Leanna's lips pressed against mine and I once again became lost. No cancer. No death. Only Leanna's lips and love.

***

My morning ritual at Mercy was pretty basic. They woke me up for breakfast. A cute nurse drew some blood. Then Kate would come in around 10am and give me the bad news.

"Your counts are still dropping." Kate stood there, a clipboard in her hands, a smile on her face.

"Well, one week into this, I suppose I should expect that." I looked at Leanna who had been camped out with me all morning.

"I do have some bad news." Kate lowered the clipboard and walked closer, but not too close. "We will need to limit your diet a little. No more greens."

"Ok." I smiled.

"Only fluids and Jell-O."

"Excuse me?" No greens, no biggy. No nothing but bland liquids. No fucking way.

"Why?" Leanna grabbed my hand, squeezing it. Calming me.

"Greens have a lot of bacteria. Jay's counts are low enough now that simple germs could kill him." Kate explained to Leanna while I just sat there.

"I'll keep an eye on him." Leanna turned to me with her eyes, her loving eyes.

"Great. The diet will start today." Kate marched out of my room.

"Um." I pierced Leanna's innocent look.

"No ums." Her face wrinkled up. "You heard her."

"Would you want to live off of freek'n Jell-O?" I laughed.

"No, but you heard what she said."

"No, I heard another rule that was meant to be broken. And it will be." I formed a grin. One that went ear to ear. Leanna giggled.

"Ok, Mr. Satan."

"Who, me?" I leaned over to Leanna's nose and rubbed mine on hers.

"Yes, you." The nose connection turned into a quick kiss.

***

Another week passed. The taste of Jell-O was too much. My counts were almost bottomed out. And I had killed the whole damn Kitty conspiracy and crippled the shadow government of Wing Commander IV. Leanna had started sleeping overnight in the chair next to my bed. Constant company.

I found it hard to sleep. It was 8am. Leanna was out like a light. I switched on VH1 and found myself watching the Top 10 countdown. Hansen. Every day. Spice Girls. Every day. 3rd Eye Blind. That wasn't so bad. But this morning it was Spice Girls first. Beautiful girls with beautiful voices. Even the videos were surreal. I gazed at the TV that lurched over me. Leanna let out a snore. Then the next video started. Hansen. I slid the TV remote/speaker next to Leanna's ear and turned up the dial on the side of the multi-purpose control.

"What the hell?" Leanna swatted air, trying to stop the sound. The sound of three pubescent teens singing a song that literally just went "Mmmbop" over and over.

I sang along out loud, holding the remote in place right next to Leanna's ear. I rocked my head back and forth, snapped my fingers and just kept singing.

"I'm going to tell everyone you like Hansen." Leanna sat up and started to laugh at me.

"This is a great song. Sing it with me!" I held the remote up in the air and waved it around.

"Closet Hansen geek." Leanna stood up and went into the bathroom, shutting the door behind her to block out the song.

"Did I miss Spice Girls already?" Leanna's voice was muffled through the hard wood door.

"Yep. But we'll watch this again at noon." I turned the volume down so I could hear her better.

Leanna came out of the bathroom. I admired the cute red shorts she had on. I was guessing no underwear, but didn't fish for the answer. "I'm going to go get some breakfast. Do you want anything?"

"A bagel." I smirked.

"Um, no." Leanna shook her head while she picked through her clothes.

"I was thinking. If I'm going to die why not let me eat what I want?" I set my bed into the sitting position. "I am dying for an egg salad sandwich."

"We'll talk about this when I get back."

The hospital room door opened and Kathy came in. "Time to wash up, Jay."

"Catchya later, Sea Monkey!"

"Enjoy the bath!" Leanna laughed.

Kathy was pretty cool to me. She brought in a basin with warm soapy water and a washcloth. "So who gets to do the deed?" I chuckled.

"I'll wash your arms, feet and legs. You can do your 'other' parts." Kathy gave me a little grin.

The door swung open again and a new face appeared. A slim, black haired beauty. Her skin was bronze. Lots of tanning for sure.

"Hi, Micky. What can I do for you?" Kathy asked.

"Kate told me that I would be caring for Mr. Libby on the weekends. I just wanted to introduce myself." She approached my bed.

Then it all dawned on me. Micky. Micky, as in Leanna's next door neighbor. Micky, whose husband was this big biker guy. Micky, who was still pretty hot. Micky who now knew my real age and could easily tell Leanna's mother.

"Jay. I should have known." Micky smiled. "When I heard the name I should have put two and two together. Leanna's boyfriend right?"

"You all know each other?" Kathy began the nice foot massage with warm soapy water.

"Leanna lives across the street." The two women chatted it up. I just sat there wondering. Am I going to get busted? At the same time I was dying?. When it was that very reason that brought Leanna and I together. I was so preoccupied with just living my life I had forgotten about the outside world.

"Well, I will see you this weekend." Micky waved and left the room.

"Good seeing you again." I smiled, waved and rested back on my bed.

"Small world, right?" Kathy rubbed my legs.

"Yep. Small world." I closed my eyes.

***

Same shit, different day. Kate's news wasn't surprising. Counts were even lower. Almost bottomed out low.

"So how long do you think it will take for them to come back up?" My heart pounded. Thumped out of control. I was looking for an answer. An answer that wasn't real.

"Traditionally once they get this low the only place they can go is up." Kate pulled up a wooden chair that had rested empty against the wall across from my bed and sat next to me.

"Cool. I'll get better in no time." I laughed.

"That's the right attitude to have." Kate took my hand in hers. "You have done an amazing job surviving this. I have talked with your doctors at NIH."

"And?"

Kate paused and took a deep breath. "They are authorizing us to do whatever we need to do to make you comfortable."

"And that means?"

"It means that if things get worse, we can break protocols." Kate squeezed my hand tight.

"I'm Jay. I don't die." I winked.

"We need to talk about a living will." It caught me off guard. I hadn't thought about it. Then again, I hadn't gotten to the point where I 'really' believed I was going to die. I felt like I might, but I hadn't accepted it. Now I had no choice. It was a real deal.

"I don't want to be resuscitated." I closed my eyes. Leanna wasn't there, thank God.

"Are you sure?" Kate pulled a piece of paper from her clipboard.

"Yes. This is my second time around. I don't plan on dying, but if I do." I grinned, "You know, happen to die. It was probably for a good reason."

"What about your friends? Family? Leanna?" Kate's voice was soft and sincere.

"Family? I left for the Navy to get away from them. Friends? I have four friends in this world. They'd understand. Leanna? She's just a kid. She has wasted so much of her life on me that it wouldn't be fair to her to draw this out any longer than need be. But like I said before, death is not going to happen." I shook my head and took the paperwork from Kate. With a flick of my wrist I signed the order to not bring me back.

***

  A couple of days had passed. Leanna had been sneaking me egg salad sandwiches and I had been soaking them up. Of course, with a solid meal comes other problems like solid stool. The toilet was cold, hard and white. I sat there. Pushing.
  "Son-of-a-bitch." I pushed until my face turned bright red.
  "You ok?" Leanna knocked on the bathroom door. The cracking of her knuckles echoed through the tiled bathroom.
  "Yep. Just a second." Finally, a painful plop in the water below. I wiped myself, but panic hit fast. Blood. A lot of it. I felt a burning sensation on my butt. The chemicals that had flushed through my system had burned my ass. Bad enough that it caused my butt to tear when I wiped. I could see blood dripping from between my legs and down into the toilet water. "Oh shit." I mumbled and jumped up, applying pressure to the wound. I quickly flushed the toilet and washed my hands. My counts were pretty much bottomed out. My platelets were low too. And now, of all stupid things, my ass was bleeding.
  "Jay?" Leanna knocked on the door again.
  I swung open the barrier between Leanna and me, smiling a devil's grin and walked carefully back to bed.
  "What's wrong?" Leanna grabbed my gown by its strings.
  "Nothing, Sea Monkey." I winked. But the wink was a false one.
  "You look scared." Leanna positioned herself in front of me.
  "Move it, Sea Monkey before I make you walk the plank."
  "Walk or ride?" Leanna giggled. I looked down. It was not a good time to be standing at attention. "Now seriously, what is wrong?"
  "Do NOT tell anyone, ok." I whispered to her, making sure that there weren't any staffers around.
  "I pinky swear." Our little fingers intertwined.
  "My ass is bleeding." I felt so embarrassed.
  "Oh, no!" Leanna pulled open my gown and looked at my naked butt cheeks. "Where?"
  "Inside." I tugged away from Leanna and sat down on my bed.
  "You need to tell Kate." Leanna looked almost as panicked as I felt.

"No." I grabbed the remote to the TV.

"Your counts are shit and your platelets are just about gone. You need to tell them or I will." The scolding look. One of cute cheeks, squinting nose and angled brows made Leanna absolutely adorable, in an angry way.

There was a knock at the door and Kathy came into the room with Dr. K. "Well how is Mr. Jason doing today?" Dr. K's voice was so hard Scottish that I almost laughed.

"His butt is bleeding." Leanna spoke up.

"What did you do?" The doctor approached me.

"Had a bowel movement." I smirked.

"Don't be wise with me. Have you been sticking to the liquid diet like I told you?" Dr. K looked almost enraged.

"Does it look like it? I think I lost another ten pounds. You should try my diet." I mouthed off to my doctor.

"If you weren't so sick I'd kick your ass for not following my orders." Kathy stepped between Dr. K and myself.

"Can we tone it down, both of you?" For a CNA, Kathy had some serious courage. While her intention was honorable, I was in a ripe mood.

"Tone what down? Is your ex-wife giving you shit again, Doc?" If Doctor K had one touchy spot, it would be his ex-wife. My step-dad warned me about K's touchiness when it came to his ex. It was the one way to set off K. That might have been a bad mistake on my part.

"You little bastard!" K barked at me and raised his hand like he was about to clobber me. Leanna backed away and Kathy did the same. "You're lucky I like your father so much or else I'd..."

"You'd what? Have a bigger temper tantrum?"

"Kathy!" Doctor K shouted. "This young man is all yours. Make sure he follows my medical orders so he doesn't die!" The mad Scotsman stormed from my room.

"Jason Libby." Leanna came over to my bed and smacked my arm. "He is trying to save you! That wasn't very nice!"

"I've never seen him that mad. You're lucky he didn't try and kill you." Kathy laughed.

"I love that man. Talk about good entertainment." I glanced up to see Hansen on the overhanging TV. "He knows I didn't mean it."

"You had better hope so." Kathy swiped the remote from my hands and turned the TV off. "That was uncalled for. He is trying to save your life."

"Yeah, having cancer doesn't give you the right to be an asshole." Leanna dug into me.

For the next few minutes the two ladies read me the riot act. Back and forth they went on how mean I was to Doctor K. I didn't think it was going to end. But Kate saved me. Well, sorta. She entered my room, clipboard in hand and an IV bag rocking back and forth.

"I see you mentioned his ex-wife." Kate had a good smile going.

"He was really mean to the doctor." Kathy responded.

"You do know you are the one and only patient who can get away with that. Doctor K cares about you a lot." Kate began switching out IV bags. Kathy flushed my lines. The taste of saline crawled up my nose. I started to feel sick.

"I know. I just needed a laugh."

"He also said your butt is bleeding. Roll on your side and let me see." I had been through a lot, embarrassment, pain, and other unfriendly things, but having to show my ass to my nurse. Well I wasn't really in for that. I turned on my side, moving the IV lines from my neck over my shoulder and opened up my gown. Kate pulled out some latex gloves and I could feel her fingers pull my butt cheeks apart.

"And?" I grumbled.

"Well, you are going to have some issues. We'll need to keep an eye on you. This could get infected quickly." Kate popped off her gloves into a nearby wastebasket. "Dammit, Jason! You can't fight off anything right now. Do you want to die?"

"Do I have to remind you…"

"Don't even say it." Kate left me sitting there, exposed.

"Are you happy now?" Leanna started to gather her things. "I'm going to go out for a while. I'll be back later."

"Don't be mad, Sea Monkey." I didn't want to be alone. Kathy snuck out of the room while Leanna leaned over and kissed me.

"I'm not. I love you too much to be mad."

***

The clock was ticking.

"They shouldn't drop any further." Kate assured me.

The next day.

"Maybe a little lower, but they should even out here soon."

Another day.

"This should be it." Kate would smile.

And the day after.

"They haven't gone up yet." Kate's smile went from real to semi fake. "Actually, they dropped a little more."

Even more time passed.

"Let me guess, they didn't go up?" I just sat there. I tried not to let the facts get to me. I winked. "Well, I have set a goal, to get out of here in two weeks for the movie *Event Horizon*."

"I'm not sure that will happen. But maybe." Kate looked at the calendar on my wall. "You'll need to cooperate with us."

"Sure thing."

***

There is a smell to having cancer. Maybe it's the stench of the drugs or maybe it's the lack of showering. But that smell. It lingers on you. No matter how many sponge baths they give you, that smell is there.

God I stink. I smell like hospital. I wrinkled my nose and threw the blanket off of me. I was there alone. Leanna was playing softball and god knows where my medical staff was. I looked down at my body. The muscles that had formed from the Navy exercise programs were gone. Now I was ghost white and thinning, just the form of bones. There was no hair to offer color. I looked like an albino prepubescent teen. I shut off my IV pump and disconnected myself. *I need a shower*. My body was weak. Very weak: like I had run about twenty miles in under an hour. I dropped the bed railing and swung my legs over the side. They dangled for a minute while I got the rest of myself up. Sitting up wasn't easy. My head spun a little, but determination gets you everywhere. *One for the money. Two for the show. Three to get ready and four to go!* My feet hit the hard floor, the hard cold floor. It had been about four days since I had last gotten out of bed. I thought about if I were to fall, I could bleed out due to low platelets. It didn't matter. I was a man on a mission. I was going to get my shower. I grabbed a sandwich bag that had been left over from one of Leanna's lunches and the roll of surgical tape that had been left on my IV poll.

It took me a few minutes to carefully make my way into the bathroom. The only light in my room was coming from sunlight that was barely peeking through my curtains. Instead of being smart, I walked without a chair or an IV poll to keep me upright. *I'm not some cripple. I can do this on my own.* And that I did. After carefully covering my central line site with the plastic bag and surgical tape, I turned on the shower. The sound caused me to shiver. Cold mist blew over my naked white form. Goosebumps formed and my head spun a little. *And they say I couldn't do this. God can do anything.* A huge grin formed cheek to cheek and I stepped into the now warm stream of water. It was a good feeling to be able to shower. I knew I wasn't supposed to, but that smell. I couldn't stand it any longer. I took an old bar of soap that had been left in the shower from back when I was allowed to use it and rubbed the hard surface on my skin. Very little foam formed, but it was enough. "I'm singing in the rain. I'm singing in the rain. What a glorious feeling to be happy again. I'm singing in the rain with you." It was funny. Breaking the rules. Not doing what I was told to do. Singing songs that I used to sing at Boy Scout camp.

Spinning. The water from the shower turned into a water spout. I tried to reach out to the tiled sides of the shower, but I couldn't concentrate enough. My soapy fingers slid on the smooth surface of the shower walls and I began to fall. My head was no good. I couldn't see anything other than a blur. *Shit, this is it. I'm going down. Got to think.* But thinking was hard to do. In a split second I was heading toward the floor, hard. I managed to place my face on the side of the shower to keep from free falling head-first onto the hard tile. My knees cracked down and I went limp. Water rained over my body, my dying white body.

I sat in the shower for about five minutes. I plotted different actions, but every time I tried to reach for something my arms wouldn't move. Paralyzed? My fingers wiggled. *Nope. I can still feel everything. I just can't move much.* I looked for options. The safety rail was too high for me to reach. Not to mention that I couldn't move much more than my fingers and lips. Maybe I could crawl? *No, too dangerous. I am safe here.* The emergency call button. The string that was attached to the button was next to my head, dangling, teasing and taunting me. I went to bend my arm but I couldn't. "You have got to be kidding me!" I mumbled. My voice wasn't working too well either. So much for calling for help. I leaned towards the string with my body, my face getting tickled by the damn thing. "I need help. Here we go." I turned my head a little, as much as I could so the string was resting across my lips. Using my teeth I gripped it, but I couldn't pull hard enough to set it off. Go figure. Using what was left of my strength I lunged my limp body forward. The string snapped and the alarm went off. My head smacked into the other side of the shower and I waited. Waited to be rescued.

When one thinks of being rescued, especially when naked, they want a certain type of person. I would have taken the Blonde Bombshell or Kathy. Hell, I would have gone for a male nurse. Someone who didn't have some type of outside connection with me. Not knowing who was coming made it difficult. I slumped my arms between my legs in order to give me some privacy. *Please be someone hot. Please be Leanna. Please be anyone.*

"Did you call?" That voice. "Jason?" That familiar voice. "Holy shit!" Micky's head peeked into the bathroom and her jaw dropped and her eyes got very large.

"Help me up." I murmured.

"I'll go get help!" Micky ran out of my room. Now I'm not sure if it was the fact that she knew me and I was naked that caused her to leave me there in the shower or maybe some hospital policy. But either way she looked freaked out by my situation. I cracked a smile. Leanna's next door neighbor just saw me naked. I'll never hear the end of it.

Seconds later several nurses came into the room, Kate in the lead. "Oh my God, Jason. Are you ok?" She shut the shower off and kneeled next to me on the floor. I could feel her hands checking my head, neck and other parts of my body.

"I'm sorry." My mouth could barely lip the words. "I'm so sorry." I lost it for a moment. Tears formed. Kate didn't understand the words I lipped, but she knew what tears were. She reached around me and held tight. My head flopped onto her shoulder. Resting. Comforting.

"Here." Micky reached over Kate and wrapped a towel around me.

"Thank you." Kate bundled my cold white flesh. "Jason, can you walk?"

I feebly nodded my head. My strength was slowly coming back. Micky and Kate propped me up and held both of my arms. "I'm sorry." I kept mumbling.

"Why?" Kate sounded disappointed.

"I smelled like cancer." I replied. "I'm gross."

"You're sick, Jason. Not to mention, you didn't smell." Kate sat me on my bed and lifted my legs up and onto the sheets. "You could have died in there."

"I'm sorry." I cried some more. I didn't cry because I was sick. I didn't cry because I was in pain. I cried because Kate had always been there for me and now I had done something to let her down.

"Micky," Kate looked at the CNA who was wrapping my ghost-like form with the bed linens, "can you put a note in his file that he needs two sponge baths a day and that he is no longer allowed to get out of bed."

"I'll do that right now." Micky left my room.

Kate and I just looked at each other. "This is not a good time to test your limits. You are at a dangerous stage here. One mistake and that's it."

"I know." Feeling returned to my face. "I thought I could do it."

"And you did, but at what cost?" Kate leaned over and hugged me.

"A bruised ego?" I let out a small laugh.

Kate looked at my face. "Did you hit your head?"

"No, I was quick to keep from causing any bruising." I lied. I knew that any other answer would land me tied to my bed. "My knees took the brunt."

"Ok. If you notice any bruising let me know." Kate kissed my forehead and left me there to think.

***

It all starts with a fever. Then it just goes downhill from there. I had been through a lot. Painful crapping. Shower falls. Liquid diets. Egg salad sandwiches. Fighting with my doctor and other things I dare not mention. It all was leading up to this. The end. After my shower fall I began to get sick. A low grade temp and fluid in my lungs. It was just getting better.

"Your temp is 102 degrees." Kate stepped away from me and looked at Leanna.

"I've kept him in bed like you asked." Leanna responded.

"Jason, this is not good. I just got your blood work results too. Nothing. You have nothing left." Kate paused. "Leanna could you step out for a minute?"

"Sure. I'll go get a snack." Leanna smiled, kissed my cheek and walked out.

"I thought you said it'd get better." I put my bed in the sitting position.

"I was wrong. This is really bad. Doctor K is going to pay you a visit tomorrow." Kate sat on my bed.

"So much for getting out in time for *Event Horizon*." It was happening. I was going. "And I already missed 3rd Eye Blind."

"I don't know what to tell you." Kate took my hand in hers.

I tried to say something. My response was all tears as I lost it. After weeks of possible hope, there wasn't any left. I cried. I cried hard. Kate held me as I let it all out. Six months of pent up frustration burst out of my soul and onto this woman who had played my stupid games.

"I'm sorry, Jason." Kate hugged me tight.

"I'm not dead yet." I sucked in my mucus and wiped my tears. "What do we have for options?"

"Platelet and blood transfusions every day. That's all I can think of. Maybe it'll help fight off whatever you have going." Kate replied as she lined her eyes up with mine. Her face was so beautiful in such a plain way. "That way your bone marrow can have time to make some blood cells."

"Let's do it. Let's just take this bitch to the bank and see how far we can go." I smiled. The odds sucked. But when you are going to go, do it in style.

"I'll put the order in. We'll start today."

***

That night I awoke to serious gurgling in my left lung. My skin was ablaze and my bed was soaked with sweat. I rolled to one side and grabbed a tissue. I coughed. Something came up. I spit into the tissue and looked at the dark mass carefully. It wasn't blood. It was black and fleshy. "What the hell is this?" I turned to Leanna who was fast asleep on a cot next to my bed.

"What Gummi?" Leanna sat up, all groggy.

"Look at this. I just coughed it up." I held my hand out like I was holding some type of ancient artifact.

"That doesn't look good." Leanna had a look of panic in her eyes.

***

"You're still alive Mr. Libby." Doctor K was as chipper as ever. "Good. I see you have been listening."

"How's the ex?" I taunted.

"You little shit!" That was the defining moment for us. The mad Scotsman threw his clipboard at me. It flew like a disk over my bed and into the window. Lucky for us the glass didn't break. "Your central line has signs of bacteria. I think that is what is causing your high temp!" He stormed toward the door. "I'm going to switch it out and then you will be getting a series of transfusions every day."

"Is that good or bad?" I laughed. "Hey, Doc, what is this?"

"What is what?" Doctor K stopped mid march and spun around.

I held up my tissue from the night before. "I've been coughing this stuff up all night."

Doctor K was the best. I taunted him, and he still did me justice.

"You said you coughed this up?"

"Last night and all day today." I took a deep breath and began coughing again. Another large black mass emerged.

"That isn't good." The doctor grabbed a tongue depressor and used it to remove the material from my mouth. "This looks like fungus."

"Fungus?" My step father appeared in the doorway.

"Mike, have a look at this."

"That isn't blood." My step dad looked at me funny. "Where are you getting that from?"

"My left lung, Dad. I can feel it."

"I'll have the lab run a test on this. Sit up for me." Doctor K pulled out his stethoscope and placed the cold circular flat surface on my back. "Breathe deep."

I tried. I could feel something break loose on the left side of my chest. As I exhaled even more material came up my throat. I scooped a nearby cup and spit into it.

"He's got a fungal infection in his left lung." My step dad was one of the best nurses in New England. He knew his stuff.

"I'll put an order in for Amphotericin B and if this turns out to be fungal we'll start it tonight."

"Lovely." I frowned. "Got any good news for me?"

"You're still alive aren't you?" Doctor K left the room.

"At ease disease, we have a fungus among us." My step dad laughed.

"I'm glad you are finding so much humor in this." I laughed with him.

***

The switching of the interior piece of the central line wasn't that bad. I sat there while Doctor K did his thing. The man was a true artist. A zip here. A zing there and in no time I was ready to rock and roll.

"Doctor K, I got the results from the lab." Kate broke my concentration on the good doctor. She held the clipboard in front of him while he finished up. "Looks like Mike was right. We'll start you right away on Amphotericin B. Get some Benadryl in him before you start."

"Is it that bad?" Adding another drug to keep me calm always made me wonder.

"Amphotericin B tends to be a little rough on people." Doctor K smiled.

"How rough?"

"You'll need the Benadryl." Kate rubbed my arm in a soothing way. I winked at Doctor K who smiled back at me.

"Thanks for fixing me up, Doc."

"Any time young man." Doctor K slid the latex gloves off of his fingers and tossed them into a nearby garbage can. "I'll come in a little later to see how you are going with the Amphotericin B."

***

Hell. It's supposed to be repetition, or so they say. But I prefer to think of it as a state of mind. I sat there and watched as Kate injected the Benadryl into my central line. I smiled, she smiled, we all smiled. Then I watched her hook up an IV bag to a pump. It was small, transparent and innocent looking.

"Call me if you feel anything out of the ordinary. We have to check you every fifteen minutes anyway." Kate patted my arm and walked out.

Anger. Hatred. Rage. My mind filled with uncontrollable emotion. My heart began to race. *What the fuck? I have this urge to yell at someone, to fucking snap!* I could feel myself loosing control. Fifteen minutes of brooding emotion.

There was a knock at the door and the Blond Bombshell entered. "Mr. Libby, how are you feeling?"

I had no self control. I tried to bite my lip. A tear trickled down the side of my face. "How the fuck do you think I feel?!" I screamed at her. The Blond Bombshell flinched.

"You don't need to yell at me." She snapped back.

"I can't help it. Something is wrong." I tried to pull back my anger. "Get the fuck out you blond-headed bitch!" Raw anger surged through me. "I can't stop this. Argh! What the fuck are you looking at?" I had no control over anything. The Blond Bombshell got close enough for me to swing at her. I missed. I could feel my teeth snapping and my body had strength that I had not felt in weeks.

"Something is wrong." She backed away from me in terror.

"I'm going to fucking kill you!" I sat up in bed, but my central line restrained my movement. "Get out, please. I don't know what is happening to me! Get Kate!" I grabbed my tissue box and hurled it at the nurse, missing her face. I watched the Blonde Bombshell run out and I struggled to get out of my bed. All that was on my mind was to hurt someone. Anyone who got in my way. *Stop it. What are you doing?* "I'm going to get the fuck out of here." *No, I have got to gain control.* "I do have control." *I don't have control.* I cried out like an animal.

"Jason!" Kate stormed into the room. I looked at her eyes, mine bloodshot with raw rage.

"Something's wrong. I have no control at all. Do something!" I cried out.

"We'll have to medicate him." Kate turned to the Blonde Bombshell and nodded. "Breathe easy, Jason. What is happening?"

"What do you fucking think?" I snapped. "I'm done with this. I am fucking through!" I screamed.

Kate didn't flinch. She came at me hard and fast and took me right down to my bed. The Blond Bombshell ran in behind her and slid a needle into one of my central line ports. "It's going to be ok." Kate whispered into my ear.

"I don't want to hurt anyone. Please. Stop this." I whimpered. I could feel a wave of fatigue run over my brain. I started to regain control. But sleep overtook me. "Sorry." That was my last word.

***

"So, what happened?" Kate sat there with Doctor K.

"After you gave me the Benadryl I started to just feel angry." I explained. "The next thing I knew, I had these ungodly urges to hurt people and I lost control."

"I guess you did." Doctor K chuckled.

"Is the Blonde Bombshell ok?" I asked, cringing, awaiting my lecture.

"She is pretty shaken up by what happened." Kate had a serious tone to her. What had happened the night before was bad.

"I don't want to do that again. No more Benadryl." I shook my head.

"You need something. Amphotericin B can do a number on you." Doctor K leaned over and looked at my eyes.

"Nothing. If I suffer a little, then I deserve it." I was weak. The night before had taken a lot out of me. "I don't want to ever hurt anyone. EVER!"

"Ok." The doctor stood up and shook his head. "No more Benadryl. I want him checked on every ten minutes when he is doing the Amphotericin B."

"I'll take care of it personally." Kate reassured Doctor K.

***

Amphotericin B without a calming drug is pretty rough. I sat there in my bed, Leanna holding my hand. My body trembled uncontrollably. The only light in the room was from the TV as it flickered. Shadows formed on the walls. The dead awaiting their brother.

"Jay, you are all cold." Leanna tossed another blanket on me, which I quickly threw off.

"No, I feel so hot." My teeth chattered. Even though I was suffering from extreme chills I still felt like I was on fire.

There came a knock at the door. Kate peered inside my room. "Jason, how are you doing?"

"He's shaking really bad." Leanna tried to straighten up my bed.

"It's the Amphotericin B. Jason, you really need something." Kate came in and stuck a thermometer in my mouth. Her face looked pretty grim, which is funny because she always looked really attractive.

"That bad, huh?" I smiled as my teeth chirped away.

"Up to 103 degrees." Kate shook her head. She did a lot of that during my last days. "We need to give you something to relax you."

"No. Nothing." I dug my palms into my bed and pushed myself up.

"Don't be so stubborn." Leanna scolded me.

"You weren't here for that disaster from Benadryl." I snapped back. "It was not good."

"No, it wasn't. How about Demerol?" Kate grabbed my wrist and started taking my pulse.

Demerol. One of the most addictive drugs on the market, at that time. I hesitated. "Isn't that really addictive?"

"Considering you might very well code if you stick to nothing, I'd say it's a good choice." Kate smiled.

"Yeah, coding would be bad." I wasn't dumb. I had better things to do than die. *Event Horizon* was the big one.

"So?" Leanna squeezed my other hand.

"Let's do it." I turned to her, winked and then began to tremble again.

"I'll be right back."

Demerol. What a drug. In seconds I could feel the soothing sensation that the drug provided. Calm tranquility. Heaven. Relief from the trembles. My room was no longer depressing, but another world waiting to be explored. Unlike my pot experience, Demerol floated me in just the right way. Not too heavy, not bad tasting. Just pure sensation. My fingers became my tools as I ran them down my face. The tickling sensation was euphoric.

"That good?" Leanna giggled.

"That good, Sea Monkey." I giggled back. I was at peace.

***

Near the end I didn't have many visitors. My mother was too

grief stricken and depressed to come see me. My step dad came to see me every other day. Jay was there once a week still. Leanna every day. My real dad popped in a couple times with my half sisters. But the lack of visits made me realize that I probably was near the end of whatever was going to happen. Grammy Pat would call me and swing by when she could. The only visitor I didn't have was my other grandmother, Grandma Parker. After my grandfather died, she began hanging out with the next door neighbor, Janice, who was forty years younger than Grandma Parker. My mother bitched about it constantly.

Doped up on Demerol and doing the Amphotericin B.

"Jason, how are you?" A voice echoed through my euphoric state. Janet's face popped past my door. Her face was thin, her hair fake blond, and make-up, but done right. I always thought she was attractive. "I've brought you a visitor."

"This might not be.." But Janet didn't let me finish. The door swung wide open and there was my Grandma Parker. The death of my grandfather had taken a toll on her. No longer looking fresh and vibrant, she now looked old. Her walker brushed across the hospital flooring.

Janet rushed to my bedside and shoved a flower arrangement into my face. "Aren't these beautiful?"

My heart almost stopped. I had bad allergies to flowers. Here she was with this arrangement, meant in good will, I think. But they were dangerous to me. Hell the sign on the door said no florals. Specifically it said: PLEASE CHECK IN AT NURSE'S STATION. DO NOT ENTER ROOM WITHOUT STAFF PERMISSION. LEAVE ALL FLOWERS AT NURSE'S STATION. NO HEAVY PERFUMES. Janet and my Grandmother reeked of flowery perfume.

"Get those out of my face." I tried to escape the scent which had already taken hold.

"You don't like them?" Janet asked innocently.

"Didn't you read the sign?" I tried to bark. But when you are euphoric it's hard to be cross. "I can't have flowers. They could kill me."

"Really?" I understood that Janet didn't get exactly what I was going through. She probably also wasn't aware that I had allergies.

"I have nasty allergies to flowers. Please just put them by the window." I begged. Janet gave me a look and set them down.

"So how are you feeling?" Grandma Parker asked as Janet pulled a chair up for her. The smell of her perfume was ungodly. I was beginning to choke up.

"I'm really sick. But I am glad you came to see me." My throat began to close up. This wasn't a normal response for me either. EPOCH

II had taken me to the lowest level of life. "I hate to do this, but I'm not allowed any visitors while I am going through my treatment." I pointed to my Amphotericin B baggy, hanging from the IV poll.

"It's your grandmother." Janet protested.

"Can you just call me?" I begged. I hated kicking my grandmother out. When I was a child she was always there. But now, now was different. I was actually having serious health issues and it was stemming from her perfume.

"That's rude." Janet looked pretty upset with me. But she was right. It was rude. When it was all over I would have some explaining to do, that is if I wasn't dead.

I watched Janet help my grandmother out of the chair and towards the door. "I love you. Get better soon." Grandma Parker waved.

"I love you too. Sorry about this." The door shut behind them. I sat there. Partly angry at the fact that I might very well die and I had disrespected my grandmother before I did.

The flowers they'd brought sat on the blower. I fell asleep.

***

"Jason." A voice in the distance called. Echoing. "Jason, wake up." Again. A shaking feeling. The earth was moving? "Jason, wake up!"

My eyes sprung open. Kate was standing there with Kathy. They looked slightly panicked.

"Did I miss something?" I felt pretty groggy.

"You have a temp of 105 degrees." Kate reached behind her. I looked past to see a cart of green ice packs. She grabbed one and tossed it to Leanna, who was stationed on the other side of me.

"This is going to help drop your temp." Kathy stuffed ice packs under my legs.

It was cold. Not too cold. Each pack was wrapped in a washcloth. "Is it that bad?" I laughed a little. "Putting me on ice already, huh?" I shivered a little bit.

"You are lucky we caught this when we did." Kate was serious. Too serious. In the time I had known her, she had not once had this look. Her intense facial features almost scared me.

"Who put the flowers in here?" Kathy asked as she stuffed away.

"Janet." I looked to the window. The flowers were gone.

"Well you can thank Janet for almost killing you." Kate sounded extremely pissed. "Is she a friend? Family? Employee here?"

"A friend of my grandmother's. She didn't know about the flower rule." I tried to defend Janet.

"Well didn't the person at the Nurse's station tell her no flowers?" Kate pulled my neck forward and placed a pack behind my neck.

"I think they just came right down here." I looked to Leanna who was looking pretty serious too.

"Leanna, I want you to check these packs constantly. As soon as they are melted call us and we will repack him with more ice." Kate gave Leanna the order like my life depended on it.

"I'm on it." Leanna looked at me and winked. It made me think that Leanna would probably make a great nurse someday.

"Good. Because his life depends on it." I was shocked to hear her say it. I hadn't thought that a stinking flower arrangement could put me in such a bad spot, but it did.

"His life depends on it." I echoed back at Kate like a ghost.

"This is serious, Jason." Kate couldn't help but smile. "This is it."

"This is it, doowhap! I've had it all." I began to sing.

Kate lightly smacked my arm. "Keep an eye on those packs."

***

My late night visit from Doctor K was different. He usually gave me a 4pm call to see how I was doing every other day. This time it was around 8pm and he was sitting at my bed. Leanna had gone home to take a shower. It was just the two of us. Doctor K's face looked somber.

"It's that bad?" I asked.

"Jason, I don't know what else to do. You have this fungal in your left lung that is barely improving. Your temp has been 105 degrees for four whole days. No matter how many transfusions we give you, nothing happens." I thought Doctor K was about to cry. "I'm open to anything."

"So, you are saying I am going to die?" I used the control on my bed to sit upright.

"Yes. There is nothing else I can do now. NIH has authorized me to break away from the protocols and do what I need to do in order to save you. The reality is it's too late." Doctor K grumbled.

"What about the Neuprogen?" My mind began to function. What was left of it.

"What about it?"

"The idea of the study was to see if Neuprogen could jump start my bone marrow. They gave me all this extra chemo. Why not match it with a double dose of Neuprogen?" I clapped my hands together. While I may not have had the facts right about the goal of the study, Neuprogen had played a major role.

"That means more sticks and your platelets are critically low." He shook his head.

"Dump it through my central line."

"No, I can't. A double dosage of what you are getting would kill you. Through your central line it could really kill you fast." Doctor K argued.

"I am going to die anyway!" I yelled. "I will sign whatever I need to. Just give the order and let's do this!"

"It was good knowing you." Doctor K shook my hand. "I'll get the legal paperwork to your room for you to sign."

"I'm not dead, yet." I winked.

"You are one crazy kid." I watched the good doctor leave my room.

Looks like this is going to be it. The end of the line. Yeah right. A grinned formed ear to ear. Jay wasn't going to die. And if I did, I was going out in style.

***

Three days passed. Every few hours a CNA and a nurse would come in and switch out my ice packs. Once a day a nurse would come in and hook me up for a blood transfusion. Each morning Kate would come in and administer my Neuprogen. Double dosage right into my central line, right into my heart. This was the day. The day I died.

It was around 7pm when the Blonde Bombshell entered my room cautiously. She had this look of fear. I didn't blame her. The last time she ventured in to see me I threw a tissue box at her head. Behind her came Kathy with a cart of ice packs. Leanna stood up and started removing the old ice packs out of the way. I was burning up. The room was dim, even with the lights on, but I didn't let it bother me. I liked the darkness.

"Ok, Mr. Libby. Time to switch them out." The Blonde Bombshell gave me an uneasy smile as she held up a fresh pack.

"You ready?" Leanna squeezed my hand gently. I nodded.

Kathy helped prop my head up while the Blonde Bombshell placed the first pack. As Kathy lowered my head back down I got one hell of a shock. A popping sound. My back arched and I felt my heart just skip a beat. No, several beats. The room began to spin out of control and I lunged forward. Ice water poured down my back. The ice pack had burst.

"Oh my God!" The Blonde Bombshell fished for a towel frantically.

"Argh!" I screamed as I tried to escape the raw cold.

"Are you ok?" Kathy used my blanket to wipe me off, but I couldn't support my weight and crashed back onto the bed.

"That was COLD!" I laughed. A laugh. I had a lot of those.

"I am so sorry!" The Blonde Bombshell seemed to almost cower for a second.

"It's ok. These things do happen." I chuckled.

"You have to admit, that was funny." Leanna smiled at me and blew me a kiss.

It took the Blonde Bombshell and Kathy about ten minutes to change my sheets while I watched, feebly from a nearby chair. Leanna kept rubbing my back, the skin ice cold. So cold, yet I was still burning up inside. Once the bed was changed they carefully helped me back under the sheets and placed the rest of the ice packs, carefully. Then the Blonde Bombshell began taking my vitals. Unlike Kate, who had a discreet way to her, the Blonde Bombshell was easy to read. I looked over at the blood pressure machine. It was pretty low. My pulse was lower. My temp still at 105 degrees. Her face was going pale.

"How am I?"

"Um, blood pressure's a little low, but nothing to worry about." The Blonde Bombshell replied as if scripted.

"Good. I'd hate to die tonight. I've got a week before *Event Horizon* hits the theatres." I held up my hand and flipped up my index and pinky. The sign of the devil.

"Well, get some rest. I'll check on you later." She sounded skeptical.

"Goodnight, Jason." Kathy rubbed her hand on my shoulder.

"Night ladies." I waved.

***

The TV had been on all night. Leanna snored away next to me on a cot that Kathy had brought in for her. I just sat there and watched the screen blankly. Finally, borede I shut it off. Almost complete darkness. Light from behind my window curtain offered me a little luminescence, not a lot, but enough. My body still felt as if it were on fire. My head became filled with nothingness. Clouded thoughts. Nothing tangible. I closed my eyes for a moment and took a deep breath. Then something caught my attention. By my hospital room door, shadows. As if all the darkness in the room had been magnetically attracted to that point. I saw movement.

Thud-ump.

As if smoke had been blown in from under the door.

Thud-ump…thud-ump… My heart racing.

The cloudy smoke began to take shape. I had seen that form before. In my nightmares.

Thud-…….my chest stopped thumping.

The Boogeyman. The one creature who'd brought me constant terror as a child. Here. Standing before me like a God.

A wheezing sound from my lungs. Air passing from me. I could feel my chest sink.

I am not scared this time. *Why? Why do I not feel fear? Terror?* It steps forward and it is now clear that this darkness is Death itself. The Boogeyman reaches out to me. Then I see a glow from my right side. It's Leanna. Sleeping. Glowing. I turn back to the Boogeyman. He is awaiting my embrace. *No.* I shake my head from side to side. "I think I have found the reason why I need to live." The Boogeyman nods in acceptance of my choice. Like the way he came, the shadowy figure steps back into the darkness and the form explodes into nothingness. A deep breath.

"Oh my God!" a female voice, a crashing of an IV pole and footsteps.

My eyes open. A doctor looms over me. The Blonde Bombshell is standing next to a knocked over IV poll. Her beautiful face is ghost white. A total look of panic. Leanna is clenching my hand. Tears in her eyes.

"You won't believe what I just saw." I mumbled.

"Jesus, he's alive!" The Blond Bombshell cried out.

"I saw Death." I said again, this time a raspy sound escaped making the words audible.

"Gummi, you were dead, dead." Leanna kissed my cheek.

"I'm getting the idea that is what happened." I felt different. Stronger. Like I wasn't me.

***

The next day Kate entered the room with a large smile. "You are not going to believe this!"

"Well, I died last night and I came back on my own. Hit me." I was sitting up in bed. Refreshed. Covered in weird red rashes.

"Your counts have jumped!" Kate cheered. "There is no way to explain it, but your counts have jumped a lot overnight. Even your temp is normal."

"Does that mean I'll get out in time to see *Event Horizon*?" I put on my devious grin.

"Let me check your counts tomorrow. If they jump more then yes. I don't see why not." Her tone was one of sheer joy, and it helped fill me with even more happiness.

Her visit the next day was the same. My counts had jumped again. For some reason, I was recovering at an uncanny rate. My guess was the Neuprogen overdose.

***

The following week…..at *Event Horizon*.
"Billy. Billy."
"Miller, Capt. Miller. I've got some problems here!"
"Be with me, forever"
Darkness……..
"Jay? Jay? Oh my God!"~ Leanna

The End?
I wish. Coming sometime in the future:
The Not-So-Right Way to Recover from Cancer

But first:
The Not-So-Right Way to Survive Cancer Part I

About the Author:

Jay Libby has been many things. You will be reading about his time with cancer and the time right afterwards. Since then, he started a game publishing company with one of two best friends: Jason Amerkanian. He has earned his Master's in Creative Non-Fiction Writing from Stonecoast. When he's not writing, doing art and playing Pappa with his kids, Jay spends his time teaching writing for the local college. He thrives off of educating his students about everything. Students love him and hate him, much like people did after reading this memoir. But life is best lived on the edge and that's how Jay does it. Although at the end of the day, it is his wife that saved him from total destruction by his own hands.

Would you like to have Jay come and speak at an event?

Jay Libby is available to discuss his treatment and memoir. But be warned, he isn't one to paint a picture of flowers and cake. He's up front and brutally honest, while still respecting the people around him. Since his time with cancer he has helped cancer patients understand what is going on without beating around the bush. He has watched several patients turn their attitude around and survive their illness. You can reach him at:

Jay@indirpg.com

The Not-So-Right Way to Survive Cancer Part II

www.ingramcontent.com/pod-product-compliance
Lightning Source LLC
Chambersburg PA
CBHW032140040426
42449CB00005B/325